MARY BERRY'S COOKBOOK

Also by Mary Berry

QUICK AND EASY COOK CARDS (Paul Hamlyn)
Traditional Breads and Scones
Cold Sweets and Desserts
Main Meals to Cook Ahead
Favourite Family Cakes

(ed.) BRIDE'S COOK BOOK (Vogue)

MARY BERRY'S COOKBOOK

by Mary Berry

Cookery Editor of Ideal Home Magazine

CASSELL · LONDON

CASSELL & COMPANY LTD
35 Red Lion Square, London WC1
Melbourne, Sydney, Toronto
Johannesburg, Auckland

First published February 1970
First edition, second impression May 1970

I.S.B.N. 0 304 93414 3

Filmset and Printed Offset Litho
by Cox & Wyman Limited,
London, Fakenham and Reading
370

FOREWORD

To say that cooking has changed would be an understatement. To say that things like equipment and food supplies have changed would be an even bigger one. Everything seems calculated to make life easier—supplies of fresh fruit and vegetables in the peak of condition from every corner of the world, and kitchens equipped to get the best out of them.

But the one thing that never changes is time, and that frequent race against the clock to prepare a meal. Whether she is at home looking after a young family or whether she has to rush back from work to rustle up a meal for a hungry husband, today's wife and mother just cannot find time to go to elaborate lengths with every evening meal.

In many of these recipes I have tried to show how, by making the most of canned or frozen food, it is possible to prepare several dishes without sacrificing any of the essentials of good cookery.

MARY R. BERRY

CONTENTS

CELEBRATIONS

METRIC CONVERSIONS

With the advent of the metric system the following list of conversions will prove useful:

1 kilo (1000) grammes	= 2·2 lb.
500 grammes	= 17½ oz. (approx.)
100 grammes	= 3½ oz.
1 litre = 1000 ml.	= 1¾ pints
1 lb.	= 450 grammes*
8 oz.	= 225 grammes
4 oz.	= 125 grammes
1 pint	= 575 ml.
½ pint	= 275 ml.
¼ pint	= 150 ml.

* For easier working these conversions have been approximated to the nearest unit of 25.

NOTE

Recipes that can be prepared in advance are marked with an asterisk (*). Those marked FOR THE GRAND OCCASION are more expensive but not necessarily more difficult. They are either hot dishes that can be prepared and cooked ahead and then be heated before the meal or cold dishes that can be cooked or just assembled ahead. In most cases it is best to cover them and put them in either the refrigerator or larder until they are needed.

THE KITCHEN

KITCHEN PLANNING

Decide first of all what is going to be done in the kitchen apart from cooking. Do you want to eat there? Is the washing and ironing being done in the kitchen too? Having sorted out these preliminaries the planning can really begin. Get together pictures of other people's kitchens with ideas that catch your eye, pieces of wallpaper gleaned from many sources and manufacturers' leaflets.

Then you can begin working out a plan on graph paper, which can be bought at any good stationers. Use graph paper scaled to twelve small squares to the inch. Measure your kitchen and its existing cupboards, etc., draw it to scale, and then fit in the cooker and other equipment accordingly. The question of space is often of prime importance, particularly in small houses or flats. You must consider what you have space for, what is essential, and what you can afford.

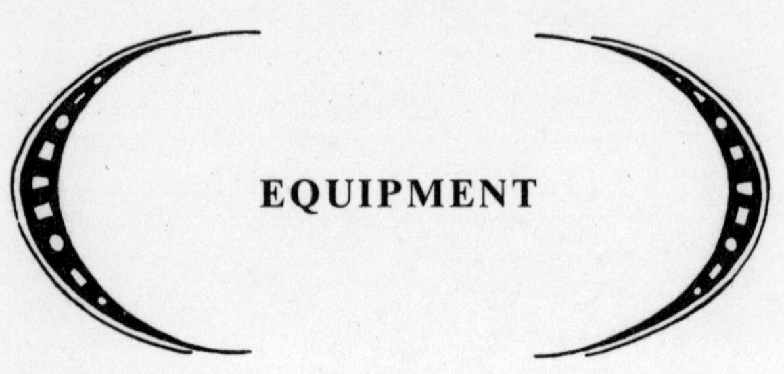

EQUIPMENT

THE COOKER

Which fuel to use is a matter of preference. Electric top cooking has advanced, and fast boiling plates are standard fixtures. New cookers have fast-heating ovens. Most of them take about ten minutes to heat up. They also cool down much quicker when turned off, leaving little residual heat. Gas, like electricity, now has thermostatically controlled ovens and automatic time control on some models.

A pre-set time clock is a boon not only for working wives but for busy housewives who want to be organized. You can put a meal in the oven, say a chicken casserole, braised vegetables and a baked pudding, before going out shopping early in the morning, then set the oven to switch on at the suitable temperature at 11.30. When you arrive home at 12.50 all you have to do is to dish up. If you are late because you are held up the oven will switch itself off.

A time controlled oven is useful for Christmas cakes too. During the day the oven may be needed for other uses or you may not find it convenient to be at home for 4–5 hours at a stretch whilst the cake is baking. The cake can be put in a cold oven the night before and the clock set to come on at six o'clock in the morning. At breakfast time you can then take over and complete the cooking.

Choose a cooker to suit your needs. If you prefer grilled food, select a cooker with a big grill. If you have a large country kitchen solid fuel will not only provide a cooker that is at the ready all the time but give a real welcoming warmth when you come down first thing on a cold winter's morning. This can, of course, be a disadvantage in a smaller kitchen in summer.

It is worth remembering that for both new gas and electric cookers you can get castors so that they may be moved for cleaning. When you've bought your cooker be guided by the manufacturer's cookery book for the shelf and baking positions in the oven.

THE REFRIGERATOR

The ideal refrigerator is wide and shallow, so that you do not have to move all the food at the front of the refrigerator to reach the things at the back. But to be practical, in the smaller kitchen it is best to choose one that is tall and takes up less floor space. Think ahead when buying a refrigerator; the tendency is to buy one too small. A good guide is to allow at least a cubic foot for each member of the family. The trend now is for larger frozen food compartments. The new refrigerators have star markings on the frozen food compartment to give guidance as to the length of time frozen food may be stored. One star means that it will store frozen food for up to one week, two stars for a month and three stars for up to three months. Some of the more expensive models have automatic defrosting.

GETTING RID OF RUBBISH

Waste is a subject that is generally not thought about until the last moment. Disposable strengthened paper or plastic bags fitted on a hinged dispenser are readily available. The new bags can be bought cheaply in bulk and take up little space as they are stored flat.

If you are choosing a plastic rubbish bin make sure it is big enough and is an easy shape for cleaning.

An electric waste disposal unit fitted in the sink will deal with most food refuse, but doesn't cope with cans, plastics, string, china, glass or cartons. It is certainly a joy for people in flats and for those with a large family.

STORAGE OF EQUIPMENT—FROM CHINA TO PANS

Keep everything as near as possible to where you are going to need it. Shallow adjustable shelves are better than deep ones for most storage. Why not stack your china on 10-in. shelves just the width of a dinner plate so that nothing gets hidden behind the things at the front?

Cupboard with different width shelves

If you don't like the sight of dishes draining and drying on the draining board have a custom-made louvred-doored cupboard with plastic plate racks inside with a tray to catch the drips underneath slightly overlapping the draining board. You can buy this ready made but a shallow bottomless cupboard with double doors which goes over the sink (*see* page 7) would be equally suitable. Everyday china can then be left in the cupboard to dry and be ready for the next meal.

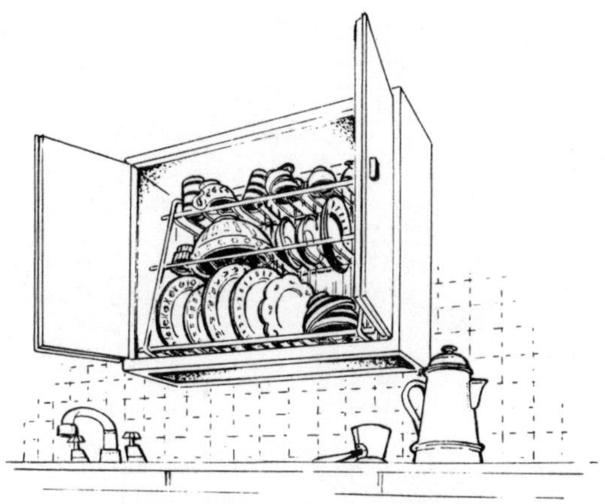

Plate-rack cum cupboard

To avoid clutter on the windowsill put the washing-up mops, cloths and brushes, also cleaning agents for washing-up, in two plastic racks fitted to the door below the sink. The washing-up bowl can go on the floor of this cupboard and alongside this put a rack for washed milk bottles.

Utensils stored inside cupboard door

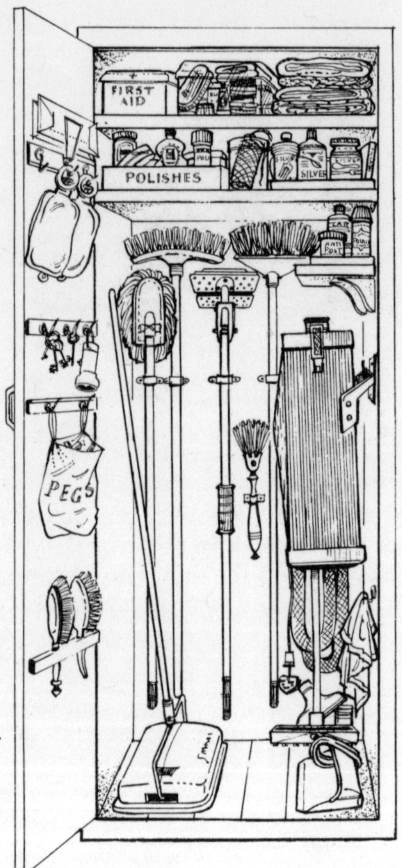

Broom cupboard

Other cleaning agents can be kept on the narrow shelves in a tall broom cupboard.

If you have the choice have two shallow drawers with compartments for knives, spoons, spatulas and things, in preference to one deep one. The compartments can be bought divided into trays which, of course, are removable for cleaning.

A shallow cupboard by the table that is used for breakfast is very useful. On the top two shelves you can keep every kind of jam, honey, pickle and sauces, and on the lower shelf cornflakes, sugar, biscuits, breakfast and morning coffee china. If you are feeling lazy you can then stretch from a sitting position for everything!

Pans can be kept in deep drawers, or in a cupboard near the stove with lids on a rack hung on the door.

Vertical storage for baking trays, meat tin, swiss roll tins, chopping board, cooling rack and bun tins takes up less room; the divisions can be of hardboard. If they are painted black they don't show either scratches or dust.

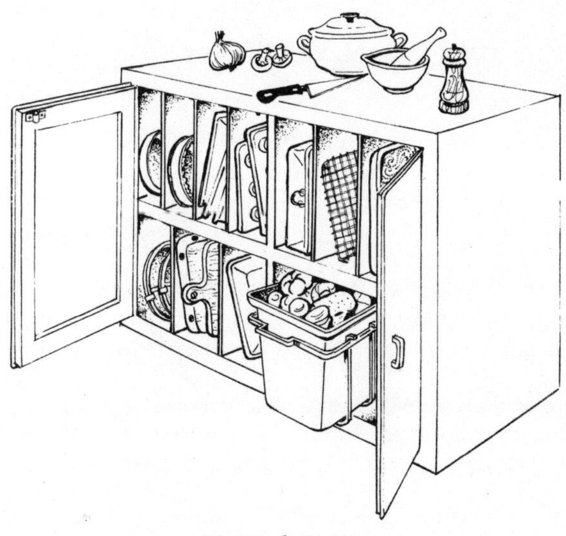

Vertical storage

If you are choosing ready-made cabinets, the main point to bear in mind is what you propose keeping in them.

NOT NECESSITIES BUT WELL WORTH CONSIDERING

DISH-WASHING MACHINE

We are reminded frequently by clever advertisers how many hours of our lives we spend toiling at the sink. The best dish-washers wash most things better than by hand, such as the ones that have front opening which makes for easy loading. As the plates have to be scraped before being loaded into the machine it's as well to fit the machine next to the sink and near the rubbish bin. If possible, have the machine permanently plumbed in, or have separate taps so that the sink can be kept free for other chores.

ELECTRIC MIXERS AND BLENDERS

Electric mixers are mainly in two sizes. The small portable ones with a whisk that you may hold in the hand for creaming cakes, whisking sponges and restoring a lumpy sauce in the pan to smoothness, usually can be fitted to a stand too. The disadvantage of these is that most of them haven't facilities for adding attachments such as a mincer, shredder, blender, potato peeler and what have you. These larger ones have bigger motors with usually more choice of speed, can cope with heavier mixtures, and you can add attachments later.

Choose a well-known make, and have a demonstration first. When you set it up in the kitchen keep it out and have the attachments near at hand so that you use it from the start.

DEEP FREEZE

If you live far away from shops or have a productive vegetable garden, a deep freeze is a blessing. Although somewhat of a luxury it is extremely convenient. You can always have extra bread, butter, a prepared dish say of steak and kidney pie in stock, so that should there be an influx of guests you have a bank to draw from, so to speak, at short notice. Naturally enough you have to allow time for the food to thaw out.

For the large family, batch cooking can be done in advance. If you are presented with a whole salmon and there's no one at home to eat it, you can wrap and freeze it for a special occasion.

Most freezers are top opening to avoid the penetration of warm air though the easiest to load are the side-opening ones. If you have a large family, and do a lot of deep freezing, a freezer over 12 cubic feet is a good buy because it is exempt from purchase tax.

TOOLS AND GEAR OF THE TRADE

A COMPREHENSIVE LIST

Buy the best you can afford. Start with the essentials and build up as you go along, adding later such things as a thermometer, larger pans, a conical strainer, jelly moulds, deep fat pan and basket.

Electric Kettle	Is an investment to buy a good one, preferably chromium, which switches itself off when it comes to the boil.

Saucepans

Good heavy aluminium ones are suitable for all fuels. They are not glamorous but will last. A thin saucepan is a waste of time. Another suitable material is stainless steel, though it is almost impossible to find a stainless steel that really is stainless.

Four saucepans is the best number to start with, including one 8-in. size fitted with a steamer, plus a small light non-stick one for milk. A shallow pan is especially useful for making sauces. A non-stick frying-pan is an asset as well as an old-fashioned iron one.

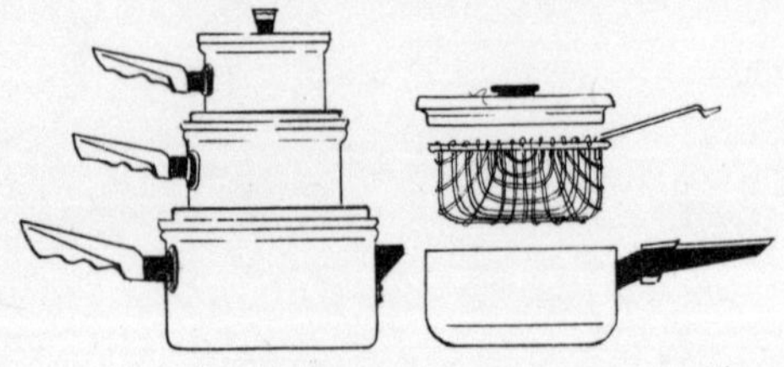

Can Opener

A stainless steel, wall-mounted one with a rubbish bin near at hand in which to throw away the lids is ideal.

Kitchen Tool Set

Including a ladle, palette knife, potato masher, fish slice and large spoon hung near the cooker is useful and saves space in the cutlery drawer.

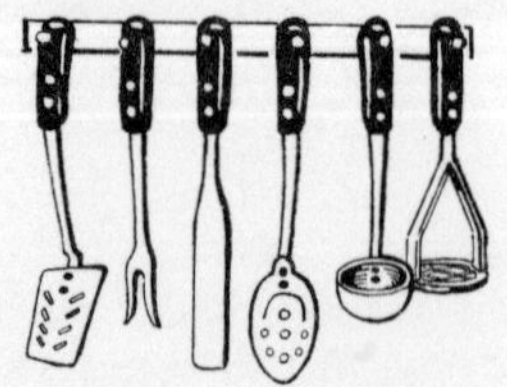

Saltbox & Peppermill Keep both these by the cooker. It will save a trip to a cupboard.

Egg Poacher This is something most people have but eggs can be poached satisfactorily in a shallow pan of water.

Pressure Cooker Useful for jam making, bottling and speeding up things that are best cooked slowly, such as casseroles, stews and stock making. This is something that can be bought as time goes by.

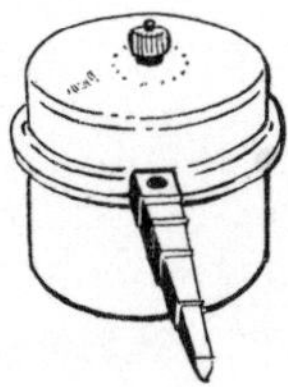

PREPARATION TOOLS

Knives Small vegetable preparation knife.
Cooks' knives—1 × 4 in. and 1 × 10 in. blades.
Bread knife.
Round-ended small palette knife for spreading.
Small stainless sharp knife for cutting up fruit.

Spoons Wooden spoons. One bowl-shaped and one straight-ended for stirring mixture in saucepans right in the corners.

Cutlery for Kitchen Meals and Tasting Knives, forks and spoons as required.

Whisks Rotary stainless whisk.
Small wire balloon whisk.

OTHER HAND TOOLS

Colander With two handles. Aluminium or stainless steel will last longest.

Sieve	One large, one small. Stainless steel for preference.
Coffee Strainer	
Grater	Four-sided stainless steel.
Skewers	A selection.
Flour Dredger	
Fluted and Plain Pastry Cutters	If you don't want to bother with these use up-ended glasses.
Pastry Brush Kitchen Scissors Potato Peeler Apple Corer Corkscrew Bottle-opener	Well worth buying the best.
Rolling-pin	Wooden without handles.
Bean Slicer	The one that you slide a runner bean through, cutting it lengthways in three slices, is cheap and highly efficient.
Lemon Squeezer	A white plastic one which catches the juice underneath is ideal.
Pie Funnel	
Baking and Oven Equipment	Large meat and Yorkshire pudding tin—these may come with your cooker. Baking sheets—two or three heavy ones to fit the oven. Bun trays: one nine-hole and one twelve-hole. Cake tins: 6 in., 7 in. and 8 in. Sponge sandwich tins: two 6 in. or 7 in. Swiss roll tins: two 7 in. × 11 in. Flan ring or tin: one 8 in. Wire cooling racks: two about 8 in. × 12 in.
Measuring	One set scales—again buy good ones. The ones with weights are best. One set plastic measuring spoons. One half-pint measuring jug. One pint measuring jug.

Mixing	One 12-in. mixing bowl—oven glass. Set of oven-glass pudding basins—$\frac{1}{2}$ pint, $\frac{3}{4}$ pint, 1 pint and 2 pints.
Pie Dishes	Oven glass—one $1\frac{1}{2}$ pint and one 2 pint or more.
Enamel Pie Plate	Two 8 in. for plate pies.
Casseroles	Two: one large and one about two pints. This is very much a matter of what you like. Earthenware are the cheapest but care is needed in their use as they break easily. Cast iron and enamel ones that you can use on the top of the cooker and in the oven are probably the most satisfactory. The non-stick ones are easy to clean and look attractive.
Ringer Timer	For up to four hours.
Storage Jars	For dry goods and spices.
Breadbin/Breadboard	
Cake Tins	For storing cakes.
Plastic Containers	For refrigerator—a selection.
Thermometer	This I wouldn't be without for jam making, fat temperatures and sweet making.
Mincer	

EXTRAS FOR KEEN COOKS

Preserving Pan or 14-pint Saucepan

Two 9-in. Sandwich Tins for family occasions

9-in. Square Cake Tin

9-in. Metal Ring Mould, Jelly Mould

Soufflé Dishes	Individual $\frac{1}{4}$ pint, one and two pint.
Conical Strainer	For straining sauces and soups.

Decorating and Icing Pipes — ½ in. plain one for piping éclairs. Large rose pipe for piping potatoes or cream. Selection of small icing pipes.
Also large and small nylon forcing bags.

Sugar Dredgers — Icing and castor.

Larding Needle — For threading strips of fat bacon through lean meats.

Trussing Needle — For sewing up birds and meat.

Storage of small boxes and tins

BUILDING UP A STORE CUPBOARD

The store cupboard should be cool and well ventilated. Shelf arrangement depends on the space available but shallow shelves are best, as things don't get hidden at the back. When placing foods in the store cupboard keep the taller items at the back, smaller ones at the front so that you can see at a glance what is in store. All those very small boxes and tins—containing herbs and spices, also colourings—can be kept together on a tray or tin lids, then when needed they can be lifted out complete (*see* page 16). The same idea goes for packet soups, packets of gelatine or blancmange—these can stand upright in a deeper box or tin which stops them toppling over frequently.

USING THE REFRIGERATOR

Use the manufacturer's instruction book. It will tell you special points about the operation of your model. For example, how to defrost it, how to clean it—different manufacturers use different materials for the lining of the 'fridge. It will also tell you the procedure for making ice cream.

Only use the refrigerator for really fresh foods. It will not make poor foods good but it will preserve the quality of good food.

Make sure all foods are cool and covered before putting them in the refrigerator. If hot, uncovered things are put in the refrigerator the ice compartment will quickly become frosted up. Also if foods are not covered the mild ones, such as butter or cream, pick up the stronger flavours of say, melon or fish. Use plastic refrigerator boxes, moisture-proof material such as plastic bags, plastic wrap, or foil.

Take cooked foods that are being served cold and cheese out of the refrigerator half an hour or so before they are needed so that they can regain full flavour at room temperature.

The coldest part of the refrigerator is under the ice-making compartment—so store raw foods such as meat, poultry, fish and bacon here.

ABOUT THE LARDER

As refrigerators get larger the larder gets smaller.

A larder is still useful and indeed ideal for keeping things that have to be kept cool but not cold, like vegetables, fruit, butter for spreading, cheese, opened jams and preserves and cooked dishes.

The old-fashioned walk-in larder with marble or slate shelves was a good invention—this is now a rare sight and we have more often than not to make do with a glorified cupboard.

If possible, the larder should have a north aspect and be well ventilated. It is a good idea to have shelves of various widths and different spaces apart for different-sized containers.

Cover the shelves with a durable, easily cleaned surface such as laminated plastic or self-sticking plastic sheeting. Failing this, surplus linoleum will do but be careful not to allow it to get wet underneath—otherwise it will quickly rot.

THE STORE CUPBOARD

The following is a mammoth check list for the store cupboard. Every household has different needs, dependent to a large extent on the type of cooking you do, so this is just a list to choose from—it is useful to have this by you when making a list for the grocer.

For Baking	Notes on buying and storing
FLOUR: Plain Self-raising Wholemeal	Keep no longer than six months. The raising agent in self raising flour decreases its action rapidly after this period.
Cornflour Baking Powder Cream of Tartar Bicarbonate of Soda	Buy small amounts and keep airtight
DRIED FRUIT: Currants, sultanas, raisins, prunes, apricots, figs and dates	These keep for three months in original packets. If keeping longer transfer to airtight jars.
Candied Peel	Buy small amounts. Keep in original cartons or in lidded glass jars.
Glacé Cherries Glacé Pineapple Chocolate Vermicelli Cooking Chocolate Sugar Cake Decorations	Buy small amounts. Keep wrapped in foil or transfer to lidded glass jars.
NUTS: Almonds, Walnuts, Hazel, Brazil	Buy whole for decoration. If you have a grinder or blender you can use this

	for roughly chopping. Ground nuts quickly lose their flavour even when stored in airtight containers, so buy small quantities.
SUGARS: Caster, granulated, lump, demerara, soft brown, icing	Keep dry and buy icing and brown sugars in small amounts as they go hard after two months.
Desiccated Coconut	Buy small amounts. Keeps up to six months once opened.

Preserves

KEEP ALL PRESERVES COOL

Jams/Marmalade Mincemeat Black Treacle	All these keep well.
Honey/Syrup	These tend to crystallize if kept too long
Chutneys/Pickles	Keep well for two years or so, buy large jars.
Mayonnaise/Salad Cream/ Home-made Preserves	Once opened keep in the refrigerator.

Use up jams, jellies and chutneys and pickles before the season comes round again. Home-made mincemeat will keep a year or more if not too much apple is included in the recipe.

Yeast, dried	Keeps up to six months once opened. Keep airtight.

Hot Drinks

TEA: China, Indian, Ceylon	Buy small amounts, and keep airtight.
Coffee Beans	Keep well—buy 1 lb. at a time and grind your own.
Coffee, Ground	Buy in small quantities and use quickly.

Coffee, Ground—Vacuum packed	Keeps well if sealed. Once opened use quickly. Ideal to have in stock.
Instant Coffee	Keeps well. Once opened use up within three months. If you use a lot of coffee buy the catering size and decant into a small tin or a glass jar.
Cocoa Drinking Chocolate Patent Milk Drinks	Keep well—once opened use within three to six months.

Cereals/Pasta/Pulses

Cornflakes and other breakfast cereals	Buy small amounts.
Porridge Oats	Once opened use within three months.
Rice—Short-grained for puddings, refined long-grained for savoury dishes	Keeps well.
Spaghetti/Noodles/ Lasagne and Vermicelli	Keep well.
Split Peas Lentils Kidney Beans	Keep well.
Semolina/Ground rice Arrowroot	Once opened use within six months.

Canned Foods

STORE CANS IN DRY CUPBOARD AWAY FROM HEAT

MEATS: Corned Beef, Luncheon Meat, Lambs and Ox Tongue, Frankfurters, Pâtés, Stewed Steak, Whole Chicken, Minced Beef	Keep two years.
Boneless Ham	Keeps six months.

FISH: Salmon, Tuna, Sardines, Pilchards, Shellfish, Herrings, Herring Roes, Anchovies, Lobster, Crab	Keep two years.
SOUPS: Consommés, Normal and Condensed	Keep two years.
VEGETABLES: Canned and quick dried Peas, Beans: various, Carrots, new Potatoes, Celery hearts, Beetroot, Tomato purée, Sweetcorn, Corn-on-the-cob, Mushrooms: button/creamed, Petit-pois, Asparagus, Artichoke hearts, Pimento, Bean sprouts, Sauerkraut	Canned keep two years. Dried keep for longer if unopened in the original container.
FRUITS: Pears, yellow and white Peaches, Raspberries, Oranges, Grapefruit, Mangoes, Lychees, Guavas, Morello cherries, Pineapple rings/chunks, Apple purée, Mandarin Oranges	Keep—one to two years.

Meals in Cans

Steak and Kidney Pies and Puddings Meat Stews Ravioli	Keep two years. Meat stews can be made more substantial by adding pastry crust or pasta.

Puddings in Cans

KEEP ABOUT ONE YEAR

Fruit Purées packed as baby foods	Used as sauces or basis for a fool.

Creamed Rice	To go with fruit or as start of Condé.
Steamed Puddings	Useful for the very hungry.

Cheese

Danish Camembert	Keeps two years—next best to the real thing—ideal to produce for the cheese-board for an emergency.

Bottles

Oil	Keep cool. Be careful not to mix salad and cooking oil. Cooking oil should be strained after use.
VINEGAR: Distilled malt (clear), Tarragon, Cider and Wine	Brown malt vinegar is very acid and strong. Distilled clear vinegar is better for general use. Tarragon, Cider and Wine either red or white, for dressings and sauces. All keep well.
Colourings	Keep indefinitely. Yellow, red, blue and green most useful. Other colours may be made from these.
Gravy Browning	Keeps indefinitely. Be sure to clean off drips after use, as the marks spread on surfaces easily. Inexpensive.
Soy Sauce	Keeps well—use for Chinese dishes.
Preserved Stem Ginger	Keeps well. Use as topping for coffee cakes, chopped in desserts or neat with cream as a dessert.

Dairy

Evaporated Milk	Keeps well. Use for chilled desserts.
Condensed Milk	After a year begins to darken and crystallize.
Patent Dried Milk	Keeps well. Once opened use within three months. When reconstituted use as fresh milk.

Cream—canned	Keeps well.
Long-life Milk and Cream	Use milk within five months, cream within three months. Chill before serving—next best thing to fresh milk and cream.
Custard Powder	Packets keep three months. Canister keeps six months.
Gelatine	Keeps well if airtight and dry.
Packet Jellies Packet Soups Packet Sauces	All these keep well. Useful for unexpected events and speeding up classic recipes.
Cake Mixes Pudding Mixes	Good to have on hand 'in case'.
Poppadums	In tins keep well—serve grilled or fried. Go with curries.
Dried Vegetable Flakes	These are useful when only a small amount needed for flavouring stews, sauces and soups. Keep well.
Bouillon and Stock Cubes	These now have largely taken the place of home-made stocks. Two most useful flavours, chicken and beef. Keep well.
Powdered Garlic/Onion/ Celery	Keep in original bottles or containers. Use sparingly.

Essences

ALL KEEP WELL

Coffee Essence	Keeps indefinitely—use for flavouring icings, cakes, cold drinks and desserts.
Oil of Peppermint	Stronger and better than essence of peppermint.
Almond	Use for flavouring almond paste, macaroons and biscuits.
Vanilla	Use for custards, fillings and desserts. Mix with coffee essence for caramel flavour for icings and fillings.
Anchovy	Use sparingly for fish dishes.

HERBS

It is fun to grow your own herbs; these popular varieties listed below once planted go on from year to year with the exception of parsley which is best grown from seed, a sprinkling every three months or so for a supply all the year round. Don't make the mistake of planting herbs at the bottom of the garden, it is far easier to have them by the back door if possible, so that you can just dash out and snip without any effort. Flat-owners should try cultivating a window-box. For the not so keen gardeners, go to a delicatessen or supermarket with a quick turnover and buy either the dried or powdered form. Store in dry atmosphere in small airtight containers.

Parsley	Dried parsley isn't satisfactory and is a far cry from the real thing. Grows from seed easily. Takes time to come up. Fresh parsley is sometimes to be had from the greengrocer.
Mint	Not very satisfactory dried. Fresh available from late spring through till late summer. Use for mint sauce, add a sprig to fruit salads and chilled summer drinks. Spreads like wild-fire in the garden. Best to grow in butt or fenced corner.
Sage	For sage and onion stuffing is the sole use in my kitchen. Easy to grow though the dried is very good.
Thyme	Common or lemon varieties used in stuffing and for meat, fish and poultry dishes. Easy to grow—dry it yourself for use in the winter months.
Rosemary	Goes well with lamb and chicken. Put a fresh sprig or a sprinkling of dried inside a chicken or under a roast joint of lamb before roasting.
Chives	Bright green with a delicate onion flavour. Add to scrambled eggs, omelettes, French dressing, sprinkle over salads and soups. Likes to be cut and cut again between late spring right through to summer. Best fresh.

Bay	Use dried—cheap to buy so no need to have a shrub yourself unless you have the space. Use only one or two leaves in savoury dishes, soups, stews and casseroles.
Horseradish	The peeled and grated root has a hot pungent flavour. Use for horseradish sauce. Jars of grated and dried powdered horseradish are available to buy. Grows easily from root but spreads rapidly and is apt to overrun the garden.
Garlic	Use very sparingly. The cloves must be very finely chopped, crushed or pressed through a garlic press. Most-used herb on the Continent for savoury dishes and salads. Dried garlic powder and garlic salt are good substitutes—again use sparingly. A suggestion of garlic is far better than overpowering the dish and frightening people off. Grow each year from the cloves.

These are some of the less usual herbs—all are available in the dried form.

Dill	A great favourite in Scandinavian countries, the fine feathery leaves are excellent chopped with cucumber salad, added to new potatoes with butter, and with egg and fish dishes. Satisfactory dried—grow from seed each year. The seeds are also used for flavouring pickles.
Fennel	A stronger version of dill. Add chopped to fish dishes.
Marjoram	(In Italy wild marjoram is called oregano, which is often mentioned in recipes.) Use the leaves sprinkled in savoury dishes, especially stuffings and meat sauces.
Basil	A herb popular in France and Italy. Use the chopped leaves sprinkled in hot or cold tomato dishes and salads.

Borage	Grows wild in this country. The leaves and blue flowers are used in summer fruit cups and chilled drinks.
Chervil	Has a flavour of aniseed. The fresh feathery leaves are useful for decoration for buffet dishes. Used chopped in sauces such as béarnaise and in vegetable dishes.
Tarragon	Grows as a tall green plant with narrow leaves, used to flavour vinegar, chicken dishes, and salads. To flavour vinegar at home just put a few sprigs in a mild vinegar.
Bouquet Garni	Frequently pops up in recipes. It is literally the French for faggot. The traditional ingredients are parsley, bay leaf and thyme tied up in a bundle and used together with peppercorns, mace and so on, added to stews, stocks and savoury dishes. These can be bought dried in muslin bags by busy people.
Mixed Herbs	A ready-blended mixture of herbs useful for keeping in the store cupboard. Use sparingly, a pinch to a ¼ teaspoon is usually plenty.

SPICES AND SEASONINGS

Nearly all spices are bought in powdered form. Buy small quantities at a time as they lose pungency on storage. Keep in the dark and in tightly closed drums or containers. Whole spices keep well and those who are fanatics can grind their own. When using such spices as whole mace, cloves, etc. and not straining stock it is easiest to tie them up in muslin and take the bag out before serving. This will save you routing around just before the meal.

Allspice	The berry of the allspice tree. Has pungent, hot aromatic flavour. Use ground with tomato and meat dishes. Do not confuse with more usual mixed spice.
Cayenne Pepper	Very hot ground red pepper made from

	chillies. Used with cheese, meat dishes, and for chutneys. Be careful to taste before adding too much.
Paprika Pepper	Looks like Cayenne pepper but is made from ground mild Hungarian peppers. Adds a touch of colour quickly; a sprinkling on top of egg mayonnaise or a sardine savoury makes all the difference. Used in meat dishes and as a basic ingredient for Hungarian goulash.
Cinnamon	Is the bark of the cinnamon tree. Bought in sticks or ground. A piece of cinnamon stick is used to flavour Glühwein and other hot punches, also for spiced fruits. Ground cinnamon goes well with apples, and is sometimes blended with dried fruits for cakes and biscuits.
Cloves	Is the dried flower bud of a tropical shrub. Used whole or ground in apple, ham and other sweet and savoury dishes. Also bread sauce. When using whole cloves remember to remove them before serving.
Curry Powder	A bought mixture of ready blended ground curry spices. Choose a well-known make. Use for curried dishes. Add a suggestion to French dressing for a change. Use with blended mayonnaise to coat hard-boiled eggs as part of a salad or starter.
Ginger	The root of the ginger plant has a hot pungent flavour. The fresh green root bought from special oriental shops is used in Chinese cooking and in chutney making. The dried whole root is used in chutney and pickle making. Ground ginger is used for gingerbread, other cakes, puddings and biscuits. The stem of ginger is also grown underground and is used for preserved and crystallized ginger which is commercially produced. Goes well with coffee and orange flavours, useful for topping cakes.

Mace	Blade mace is the outside husk of a nutmeg, and the flavours are similar, mace being the stronger. Can also be bought ground. Use with herbs for stocks, sauces and tomato and meat dishes.
Mixed Spice	A blended mixture of ground spices including cloves, cinnamon and nutmeg. Used in rich fruit cakes, spice cakes, biscuits and puddings.
Mustard	Mustard powder is ground mustard seeds with a small percentage of ground spice and wheat flour added and is packed in tins. Cold water is best for mixing and the full flavour does not develop until after a few minutes. It loses pungency if left in the pot and should be mixed for each meal. Made mustard referred to in recipes means freshly mixed mustard powder. Prepared mustard means that bought in jars and tubes, such as ready-mixed English mustard, French and other mustards. Mustard is a natural with boiled and roast beef, with bacon, for mustard sauce to go with herrings and mackerel. Use also to add piquancy to savoury sauces and dressings. Mustard brings out the flavour of cheese in cooked cheese dishes.
Nutmeg	The hard nut-like seed of the nutmeg tree. Use ground or finely grated to flavour meat pâtés, cooked meats and brawn. Good in white sauces, in cakes and biscuits. Sprinkle over milk puddings and baked custards.
Pepper	Ground from either white or black peppercorns which are the seed of the pepper plant, white peppercorns being the inside of the black peppercorn without the dark outer coating of the seed. Both can be used ground, though black pepper freshly ground preferably just before using from a peppermill tastes much better. Some people prefer to use

white pepper for all white and pale sauces. I like the speckled look—it is just a matter of preference. Whole peppercorns are used for marinades, pickling, stews and casseroles. Remember to remove the peppercorns before serving.

Saffron — Comes from the stamens of the saffron crocus. Used for flavouring and colouring cakes, breads and savoury rice dishes. The dried stamens look like yellowish fine tobacco. Bought from a chemist. A good pinch is enough for one dish. Soak in two tablespoons of warm water before adding, to extract colour and soften. Powdered saffron is also available and is less bother to use.

Salt — Common kitchen salt sold in blocks or bags is cheaper but clogs together if in a damp atmosphere. Table salt is easy to pour and is best for table use.

Seasoned Salts — Such as garlic, celery and onion salt. These have their uses but I find the dehydrated ground powders of these without salt better and more economical—after all one can add salt easily enough.

Vanilla Pod — Is the dried pod of a tropical orchid. The dark brown vanilla pod can be kept in a screw-topped jar of caster sugar, and the vanilla-flavoured sugar can then be used for biscuits and cakes or custards. The usual way of buying vanilla is in essence form for flavouring sweet things.

WEIGHING AND MEASURING

Always measure your ingredients accurately, whether with scales or measuring spoons.

A set of four plastic measuring spoons is helpful with smaller quantities of food, invaluable for spices, but keep it away from heat. When filled till level they measure one tablespoon, one teaspoon, half a teaspoon and a quarter of a teaspoon. For measuring flour for sauces it is easier to remember 1 level tablespoon = ½ oz. than to use scales.

I find a sugar thermometer cuts out any error of judgement and is invaluable when making sweets and custards or testing jam.

USEFUL TEMPERATURES

Home Freezer Storage	below 0°F
Normal Refrigerator Storage	36–38°F
Lukewarm (blood heat)	98°F
Junket sets at	98°F
Simmering	205°F
Boiling	212°F
Jam sets at	220°F
Fudge should be removed from the heat at	238°F
Chipped potatoes should be blanched in oil till soft at	385°F
Chipped potatoes should be fried till brown at	395°F

OVEN TEMPERATURES

Thermostat setting	*Approx. temperature centre oven*	*Heat of oven*
¼	225°F	very cool
½	250°F	very cool
1	275°F	very cool
2	300°F	cool
3	325°F	warm
4	350°F	moderate
5	375°F	fairly hot
6	400°F	fairly hot
7	425°F	hot
8	450°F	very hot
9	475°F	very hot

CUP MEASURES

It is infuriating when reading a recipe to be put off because one is muddled by cups. What is a cup anyway?

The British Standards Institution Cup measure is ½ pint—10 fluid oz. A full-sized teacup filled right to the brim is about half a pint, whereas the American cup is less than ours—8 fluid oz. So to clarify the situation these are the comparisons and in case you are back from the continent the metric equivalents too. If you use American recipes an American measuring cup is useful.

BRITISH MEASUREMENTS

1 British Imperial pt. = 20 fl. oz.
1 British cup is ½ pt. = 10 fl. oz.
¼ pt. = 5 fl. oz.
¼ pt. = 5 fl. oz. and also 1 gill

AMERICAN MEASUREMENTS

1 American pint = 16 fl. oz.
1 American cup = 8 fl. oz.

FRENCH MEASUREMENTS

30 grammes	Approx. 1 oz.
100 grammes	Approx. 3½ oz.
1 kilo (1,000 grammes)	Approx. 2 lb. 3 oz.
1 litre	Approx. 1¾ pints
1 decilitre	Approx. 6 tablespoons

MEAL PLANNING

PLANNING AHEAD FOR EVERYDAY MEALS

No two families are the same so naturally it is up to you to plan and cook meals to suit your own brood. Endless time is saved, I find, by sitting down with a pencil and paper and planning a batch of meals for preferably the next week or at least three or four days at a time. Think of the main meals first then any befores or afters, making the most of foods in season. Have one big bake and make bread, cakes and biscuits at one time. Work out shopping lists from these lists.

WHAT TO CHOOSE FOR A DINNER PARTY

When thinking what to have for a dinner party think first of who is coming and what they would like. Never plan dishes that must be served the moment they are cooked or ones that need heaps of last-minute attention. Carving for several people takes time and with many joints a good measure of skill too. Do warn your husband what the joint is so that he may know what he has to be up to in advance—this is if you choose a joint or bird.

Consider having a main dish cooked in an oven-to-table type dish. Have good-tempered food that does not mind waiting. Soup is an easy starter as it needs just to be heated up; a chilled one in summer too is unusual and surprisingly popular.

A FEW MUSTS FOR SUCCESS MENUS

Make the meal full of interest, with lots of colour and difference in textures. Serve what should be hot really hot and cold things icy cold. Avoid using similar ingredients in successive dishes. For example, do not start with melon, then have fruit salad for dessert or start with herrings with soured cream followed by Boeuf Stroganoff, ending up with, say, a chocolate mousse which also contains lashings of cream. Don't be over-ambitious and then feel worn out when your guests arrive. If you are a wife and have a career too the preparation will have to be done the evening before, so choose dishes that reheat well or cold ones that may be made in advance and chilled.

SAVING TIME IN THE KITCHEN

PASTRY AND CRUMBLE MIX

Make up shortcrust pastry up to the rubbing-in stage and keep it in the refrigerator in a polythene box or screw-topped jar. Then just add water for pastry and sugar for crumble.

FRENCH DRESSING

Make up a bottleful at a time and keep in a cool larder. Then add shredded onion or chives at the salad-bowl stage. Keeps at least a month.

MAYONNAISE

Make up a half pint or so at a time and keep in a covered jar in the refrigerator. Keeps for a month.

VEGETABLE PREPARATION

Peel root vegetables for a couple of meals at a time and cover with water. Keep cool. Wash lettuce and keep whole, except for the outside leaves, in a plastic box in the refrigerator or in a saucepan in a cool larder. Prepare green vegetables for a couple of meals at a time, keep covered in the refrigerator or in a cool larder, but do not slice until just before they are to be cooked. Put peas into a polythene bag in the refrigerator.

If you are chopping onions, chop a few more than you need. Wrap in a parcel of foil or pop in a washed large cream carton and keep in the refrigerator on hand for use to add to salads, dressings, casseroles and frys. If you intend to keep prepared onion for more than three days, cover it with a little salad oil first.

COFFEE MAKING

A word about coffee. There has been a lot of mystique built around the making of coffee. First use a good blend—there are excellent varieties of vacuum-packed ground coffee which are easily stored and which, when opened, have the fragrance and flavour of freshly milled beans. Use enough coffee: for most blends measure $1\frac{1}{2}$ oz. per pint of water when serving two-thirds coffee, one-third milk, with single cream or just as black coffee. In most shops where coffee is sold a measuring spoon may be bought for sixpence. Use four of these per pint or two heaped tablespoons.

There are numerous ways of making coffee, but the simplest is, I think, the best and as easy in fact as making tea. Measure the coffee into a dry, heated earthenware jug, pour on the required amount of freshly boiled water and stir vigorously. Leave to infuse for five minutes until the grounds sink to the bottom of the jug. If necessary turn the grains over with a spoon so that they sink. Strain into a well heated coffee pot, serve with hot (not boiling) milk or single cream.

When making coffee for numbers make it in advance in jugs, strain off the grains and reheat just before it is needed; or if you can make it say half an hour before serving just keep the jugs hot by standing them in a meat tin of barely simmering water. Be careful not to boil the water as then the flavour of the coffee becomes bitter and the aroma is lost.

SAVING THE DAY

Calamities happen usually just when you least expect them—maybe the phone goes when you are in the middle of making a sauce or your youngest falls down when you meant to take the cake out of the oven and the edges get burnt. So many maddening happenings but here's some encouragement on how to cope. Get moving quickly and pretend nothing has happened!

A LUMPY SAUCE

Draw the pan away from the heat—whisk it frantically with a wire whisk or tip it into an electric blender for a few seconds.

SAUCE TOO THICK

Add more liquid.

SAUCE TOO THIN

Add cornflour blended with little cold milk or water, or reduce by boiling.

SALTY CASSEROLE OR SOUP

Add a couple of tablespoons of instant potato and extra unseasoned stock.

BURNT SOUP

Throw it away. Open a can and add a few fresh ingredients such as a lightly fried onion, grated carrot or shredded leeks. Then stir in a little top of the milk before serving.

CASSEROLE OR MAIN DISH BURNT TO A FRAZZLE

Make spaghetti bolognaise in a jiffy. Open a can of minced beef, add a little garlic, small can of tomatoes, fresh tomatoes or purée, pinch of herbs, seasoning and a dash of sugar. Heat slowly till piping hot. Meanwhile put spaghetti on to boil (about 3 oz. per person). In fifteen minutes all should be well.

MAYONNAISE CURDLES

Start again with a fresh egg yolk in a clean basin then very slowly whisk in the curdled mayonnaise.

MOULDED JELLY OR MOUSSE FLOPS WHEN TURNED OUT

Whisk with a rotary whisk and turn into individual glasses. Top with whirl of cream or chopped nuts.

FLAN CASE BREAKS WHEN YOU LIFT IT ON TO THE PLATE

Put the filling in a shallow pie dish and crush the flan case and sprinkle like crumble over the filling. Then scatter the top with coarsely grated chocolate, little sieved icing sugar or sprinkling of coarse brown sugar—whichever goes best.

FRUIT GLAZE SOAKS INTO A SPONGE FLAN CASE—MAKING THE SPONGE SOGGY

Turn it into a trifle by spooning over 3 or 4 tablespoons of sherry, sprinkling over a few crushed macaroons or ratafias if you've got some, then masking the top with whipped cream. Decorate with almonds or cherries.

CREAM WON'T WHIP

Give up the ghost and serve it as pouring cream. Don't add more fresh cream, it won't help. Next time make sure it is double or half double half single and chill before whipping.

THE CAT HAS EATEN THE SPECIAL PUDDING

Take a deep breath. Open a can of peaches, tip them into a shallow oven-proof dish that will fit under the grill, spoon over a soupçon of brandy. Cover with a few marshmallows and flash under the grill until they have just begun to melt and brown—or make any of the easy puddings in pudding section.

BURNT EDGES TO CAKE OR PIE

Gently trim off burnt part with grater.

THE DOG EATS THE PÂTÉ FOR THE FIRST COURSE

Open two cans of pâté, mash them down well with a little cream, a little brandy and a teaspoon of chopped chives—lots of freshly milled pepper too. Then shape it up to a loaf shape on a flat dish and decorate the top with sliced cucumber.

FRENCH BREAD OR ROLLS ARE NOT CRISP AND FRESH ENOUGH

Sprinkle with water and place in a hot oven for 7 minutes. Serve warm.

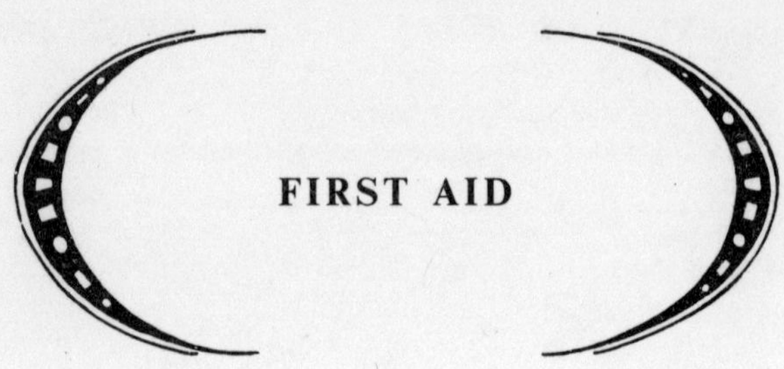

FIRST AID

Accidents happen even in the most organized happy kitchens and it's as well to know what to do about them. These are some of the most likely things that you might have to cope with. The following notes have been compiled with the help of the St. John Ambulance Association.

BURNS

Minor burns and scalds, say of the size of half a crown or less, without blistering, are annoying but not dangerous. They may be relieved by holding under cold running water. If the burn was from fat wipe this off first, to relieve the pain. Just cover afterwards with a dry dressing.

Ointments are not used in the treatment of burns nowadays.

If you have to cope with an extensive burn, send for an ambulance. Keep your casualty warm and cover the burned area with clean linen or cotton sheet until help arrives.

CUTS

These can be frightening—but keep your head. For minor cuts, gently wash and cover with a sterile dressing. If the cut is deep, press with the thumbs into wound to stop bleeding, then bandage firmly. If the cut cannot be cleaned, go to the doctor.

ELECTRIC SHOCKS

Can cause burns at the point of contact and can even strike the casualty unconscious. First, obviously, one must switch off the current. Then assess the seriousness of the accident. If a minor burn, treat for this as explained above, if a major, get help as soon as possible. In a severe case of an electric shock it may be necessary to give artificial respiration to revive the patient.

GASSING

Again, obviously, turn the gas off and get the casualty into the fresh air, before sending for help. Again, it may be necessary to give artificial respiration.

SPRAINS

Can often be avoided by using non-slip polish on the kitchen floor and taking care to mop up anything that has been spilt immediately. However, they do happen from time to time so this is what to do. At once surround the joint with layers of cotton-wool and bandage firmly. Go to the doctor. When the injury involves the wrist, elbow or shoulder, the arm should be supported in a sling.

STINGS

First remove the sting if possible, that is if it is visible sticking out of the skin. Apply an antihistamine cream. Should the sting be in the mouth, let the patient suck ice and get to a hospital or send for a doctor at once. Keep up the ice treatment until the doctor can take over.

EQUIPMENT

To treat minor injuries whether in the kitchen or in the home, it is useful to have at least this amount of first-aid equipment to hand:

$\frac{1}{4}$-yd. pkt. lint	Tin adhesive plaster dressings, mixed sizes
$\frac{1}{4}$-yd. pkt. gauze	A few safety-pins
1-oz. pkt. cotton-wool	A pair of scissors
1 1-in. roller bandage	Bottle of mild antiseptic
1 2-in. roller bandage	Aspirin or similar patent-type preparation

RECIPE SECTION

SOUPS AND STARTERS

SOUPS

Although most canned and packet soups are remarkably good, there's nothing to beat a home-made soup. I always make quite a lot at a time because it's one of those things that reheat perfectly—if you've made a soup for a dinner party on, say, Saturday or Sunday, it is most welcome again to cheer up the cold meat on Monday at lunch-time.

Tomato Soup—Post Haste!*

FOR 4

1 oz. butter; 1 small onion, finely chopped; 1 oz. flour; ½ pint milk; ½ pint water; 2¼-oz. can tomato purée; 1 level teaspoon caster sugar; salt and pepper; pinch dried mixed herbs; chopped parsley

Preparation: 5 minutes *Cooking time: about 10 minutes*

This soup is literally made in 10 minutes.

Melt the butter in a pan, fry the onion, without colouring, until soft. Stir in the flour and cook for 1–2 minutes without browning. Draw to one side of the heat. Gradually add the milk and water, stirring until smooth, then add tomato purée. Stir in the sugar, seasoning and herbs. Simmer gently for 7 minutes or until the onion is cooked. Taste and season with more salt and pepper if necessary. Serve sprinkled with parsley.

French Onion Soup*

FOR 6

2 oz. lard or good dripping; 1 lb. onions, peeled and finely chopped; 1 oz. flour; 1½ pints stock or 1½ pints water and 2 chicken stock cubes; 2 level teaspoons tomato purée; salt; pepper.

6 slices French bread, lightly toasted; 1–2 oz. Cheddar cheese, grated.

Preparation: 15 minutes *Cooking time: about 1 hour*

This soup is ideal to have before a salad for a Sunday night supper.

Melt the lard or dripping in a pan and fry the onions slowly until they are beginning to turn brown. Blend in the flour and cook it gently until it is brown, then add the stock, stirring until it is smooth. Add the tomato purée and seasoning. Simmer the soup, covered, for 30–40 minutes.

Sprinkle the slices of toasted bread with the grated cheese. When the soup is cooked check the seasoning and pour into an oven-proof tureen, arranging the slices of toast on top. Brown the toast under a grill until the cheese has melted and is just beginning to turn brown. If you haven't a suitable dish melt the cheese on the toast under the grill and float it on the soup just before serving.

Mushroom Cream Soup*

FOR 6

2 oz. butter; 1 shallot, very finely chopped; 8 oz. mushrooms, finely sliced; 2 oz. flour; 1 pint stock or 1 pint water and a chicken stock cube; ½ pint milk; 1 tablespoon chopped parsley; salt; pepper; ¼ pint single cream.

Preparation: 15 minutes *Cooking time: about 15 minutes*

This is a rich soup with chunky pieces of mushroom. If a purée soup is preferred, either put it through a sieve or pulverize it in an electric blender before adding the cream and parsley.

Melt the butter in a pan, add the shallot and fry it gently for 5 minutes. Stir in the mushrooms and continue to fry gently, stirring, for a further 5 minutes. Sprinkle in the flour, cook for a few minutes, then draw the pan to one side of the heat and stir in the stock, adding it slowly at first, and stirring all the time. Return to the heat and bring to boiling point, stirring until it has thickened. Blend in the milk, add the parsley (saving some for topping) and season well. Add the cream just before serving. Scatter each bowl of soup with chopped parsley.

Spring Soup*

FOR 6

1½ oz. butter; ½ lettuce, chopped; 1 bunch watercress, chopped; 1 bunch spring onions, chopped; ¼ pint water; 1 chicken stock cube; ¾ pint milk; salt; freshly milled black pepper; 1 5-oz. carton soured cream

Preparation: 10 minutes *Cooking time: about 20 minutes*

Melt the butter in a large pan and then add lettuce, watercress and spring onions. Cook over a gentle heat, with the lid on, for about 10 minutes to soften the vegetables. Then remove the pan from the heat and add the water, crumbled stock cube and milk. Season well with salt and pepper. Return to the heat, bring to the boil, then simmer slowly for about 15 minutes until the vegetables are tender. Then strain off liquid and sieve vegetables, adding the purée to the liquor; or put the mixture into a blender. Return to pan, heat until piping hot, pour into individual soup bowls and top with soured cream.

Chilled Avocado Soup

FOR 4

2 avocado pears; juice ½ lemon; ⅛ pint French dressing (see page 64); 1 can consommé (10-oz. size); 1 carton soured cream (5-oz. size); salt; pepper; chopped chives.

Preparation: 10 minutes

Cut the pears in half, remove the stone, scoop out the flesh, and sieve. Blend in remaining ingredients or remove flesh from pears and put into a blender with ingredients. Season well. Serve chilled in small bowls, with a few chopped chives on top for garnish.

Gazpachio*

FOR 4

1½ lb. ripe tomatoes, skinned; ½ onion, very finely chopped; 1 small green pepper; ½ cucumber, peeled; 1 clove garlic, crushed; 6 tablespoons salad oil; 3 tablespoons white wine vinegar; ½ pint chicken stock, or ½ pint water and a chicken stock cube; salt; freshly ground black pepper; finely chopped chives or parsley

Preparation: 15 minutes

A classic soup from Spain, it improves by being kept overnight in the refrigerator to let the flavours blend.

Cut the tomatoes in quarters, remove the pips and cut into ¼-inch dice. Put into a bowl with the onion. Remove the stem, seeds and white pith from the pepper, cut the flesh into ¼-inch dice and add to the tomatoes with the cucumber, cut in similar-sized pieces, and the garlic. Blend in the salad oil and vinegar, then the chicken stock. Season with salt and pepper. Leave in the refrigerator for several hours until thoroughly chilled. Just before serving divide between four soup bowls or dishes and sprinkle each with chopped chives or parsley.

Serve as they do in Spain with side dishes of diced tomato, diced cucumber and fried bread croûtons.

Chilled Watercress Soup*

FOR 6

2 bunches watercress; 2 oz. butter; ¼ lb. onions, peeled and thinly sliced; ¾ lb. potatoes, peeled and roughly sliced; 1 pint stock, or 1 pint water and 1 chicken stock cube; ¾ pint milk; salt and pepper; blade of mace; ¼ pint single cream

Preparation: 15 minutes *Cooking time: about 30 minutes*

This soup is also just as good served hot. If doing so take care not to boil the soup after adding the cream.

Trim off a small bunch of top leaves of the watercress for garnish. Melt the butter in a heavy-based pan and sauté the onion and potatoes for 3–4 minutes without colouring. Add the stock and milk. Season with salt, pepper and the mace. Simmer very gently until the vegetables are nearly cooked (about 15 minutes). Then add the watercress with stalks and simmer for a further 10 minutes. Remove the mace.

Put through a sieve or pulverise in an electric blender. Taste and adjust seasoning. Refrigerate overnight. Just before serving stir in the cream and sprinkle with finely chopped watercress leaves.

TWO SUMMER VEGETABLE STARTERS

Asparagus

Preparation: 5 minutes

Fresh asparagus is a splendid beginning for a summer dinner party. A 1-lb. bundle will serve two to three people. Trim off the white and brown jagged ends of the asparagus and cut all the sticks to an average length. Scrape off the rough skin near the cut end with a sharp knife. Wash well in cold water to get rid of any sandy grit. Boil in salted water in a large shallow pan, covering the asparagus well with water, for 12–15 minutes until just tender, then lift the asparagus out carefully and drain. A fish slice is a useful utensil for this. Serve hot with Hollandaise Sauce or melted butter or cold with French dressing.

Hollandaise Sauce

FOR 4

2 tablespoons wine vinegar; 2 tablespoons lemon juice; 2 bay leaves; 2 blades mace; 6 peppercorns; 3 egg yolks; 4 oz. fresh butter; salt; pepper

Preparation: 5 minutes *Cooking time: about 10 minutes*

There are two musts for success with this sauce. One is to make it in a basin over hot *not* boiling water and to whisk continually whilst it is cooking. Two is to keep it warm by standing it in a bowl over warm water—if the water is too hot the sauce will continue to cook and so turn into scrambled egg. So take care and then it is easy.

Put the vinegar, lemon juice, bay leaves, mace and peppercorns into a small pan and simmer until the liquor has reduced to 2 tablespoons.

Put the egg yolks into a small bowl, blend in the strained liquor from the pan and mix well. Put the bowl on top of a pan of hot, but not boiling, water, beat in a knob of soft butter and then whisk the mixture over the heat until it has thickened. Gradually add the remaining butter, whisking constantly and removing the bowl from the pan if the sauce thickens too quickly. When finished the sauce should just form very soft peaks. Add salt and pepper to taste. Keep warm by standing in a bowl over warm water until needed.

Globe Artichokes*

These are the buds of a large and handsome plant flowering in the middle to late summer in England. However, because of imports from other countries the season has been greatly extended and artichokes are now in the shops from April to November. They not only make an unusual starter but they keep everyone busy too!

Preparation: 5 minutes

Allow one artichoke for each person. Wash the artichokes well in salted water. Trim the sharp points of the leaves square with scissors, if liked, and cut off any stalk to level the base.

Cook them in boiling salted water for 45 minutes or until a leaf can be pulled out easily. Drain well. I prefer them served hot with Hollandaise sauce or melted butter, though they may be served cold with French dressing.

HORS D'OEUVRE

An hors d'oeuvre can of course be a meal in itself—but when making it a beginning to a meal it is as well to remember not to make it too large. Choose about four ideas, arrange them in individual dishes or on one large platter, then decorate with watercress, parsley, mint sprigs, lettuce hearts or perhaps radishes or tomatoes.

These are some home-made hors d'oeuvre which would go with canned sardines, shellfish or herrings. Sardines can be simply turned out of the can and sprinkled with paprika, lobster and crab masked in a pink mayonnaise, that is, mayonnaise coloured with a dash of red colouring or tomato purée. Herrings can be bought canned in a marinade or if bought as roll mops served in the Scandinavian style with soured cream.

Scandinavian Herring Salad*

FOR 4

4 pickled herrings; 1 small onion; 1 sweet apple; 2 teaspoons lemon juice; 5-oz. carton soured cream; white pepper; salt; watercress

Preparation: 5 minutes

Drain the herrings from the vinegar. Cut each herring in half lengthways and then cut each half into about 8 strips. Slice onion into fine rings. Cover the onion with boiling water and drain after 1 minute. Core and slice apple and sprinkle with lemon juice. Reserve a few apple slices for garnish. Blend rest of apple, onion rings, cream and ½ teaspoon of lemon juice. Season well. Spoon over herring pieces and garnish with apple slices and watercress.

Oeufs Aurore*

FOR 4

1 bunch watercress; 4 hard-boiled eggs; 8 tablespoons well seasoned, home-made mayonnaise or good bought mayonnaise; 2 level teaspoons tomato purée; 1 teaspoon lemon juice; dash sugar; salt and black pepper; paprika pepper

Preparation: 10 minutes

Arrange sprigs of watercress on serving dish. Cut the hard-boiled eggs in half lengthways and arrange them, cut side down, on the dish. Blend together the mayonnaise, tomato purée, lemon juice, sugar and seasoning and just before serving coat the eggs with the sauce and sprinkle them with paprika pepper.

Tomatoes Stuffed with Cottage Cheese*

FOR 4

4 large, firm tomatoes; 4-oz. carton cottage cheese; 1 pickled sweet cucumber, chopped; 1 tablespoon sweet chutney, chopped; 2 tablespoons home-made mayonnaise or good bought mayonnaise; salt and pepper; punnet of cress

Preparation: 10 minutes

Skin the tomatoes by plunging them in boiling water for about 5 seconds and then into cold water. It will then be easy to peel off the skins. Place a tomato, stalk side down, on a wooden board. With a small knife make cuts almost through to the base of the tomato to form six 'petals'. Open out the petals to form a flower shape. Carefully remove the seeds from the centre of the tomato. Repeat the process with the remaining tomatoes. Mix together the cottage cheese, cucumber, chutney, mayonnaise and seasoning. Pile the cheese mixture into the tomatoes and garnish with cress.

French Dressed Artichoke Hearts*

FOR 4

Two 7-oz. cans artichoke hearts, drained; ¼ pint French dressing (see page 64); chopped parsley

Preparation: 5 minutes

This can be part of an hors d'oeuvre or a starter by itself.

Divide the artichoke hearts between four individual serving dishes. Coat the hearts with French dressing and sprinkle with chopped parsley. Serve with thinly sliced brown bread and butter.

Taramosalata* FOR THE GRAND OCCASION

FOR 4

½ lb. smoked cod's roe; 2 small slices white bread without crusts; 2 tablespoons milk; ⅛ pint (6 tablespoons) olive oil; 2 tablespoons lemon juice; salt and pepper

Preparation: 10 minutes

If you have a blender it will make this smoked cod's roe pâté in a moment but even so it doesn't take long this way.

Remove the skin from the cod's roe. Place the roe in a mortar or bowl and pound it with a pestle or mash it with a fork until it is smooth. Soak the bread in the milk, then squeeze out as much of the milk as possible. Add the bread to the cod's roe and mash again. Add the oil a teaspoon at a time. Stir in the lemon juice and seasoning. Chill, before serving with hot toast and butter.

FRUIT STARTERS

Parma Ham with Melon*

FOR 4

6 oz. very thinly sliced Parma ham; 1 small, ripe melon; lemon wedges

Preparation: 5 minutes

Another variation on the melon theme. You can buy Parma ham at a good delicatessen. It also comes in 6 oz. cans.

Arrange the Parma ham on four plates. Cut the melon into four slices, remove the seeds and put a slice on each plate. Serve with wedges of lemon.

Chilled Melon with Prawns*

FOR 4

1 ripe, chilled melon (about 2 lb.); 4 oz. shelled prawns; 5-oz. carton soured cream; salt; freshly ground black pepper; sprigs of mint

Preparation: 10 minutes

Add the cream at the last moment otherwise it will quickly become watery.

Cut the melon in half then scoop out the flesh in balls, using a small potato scoop. (If you do not have a scoop the flesh may be cut into $\frac{1}{2}$-inch cubes.)

Divide the melon balls between four individual serving dishes and sprinkle with the prawns. Season the soured cream with a little salt and plenty of pepper and just before serving pour the cream over the melon and prawns. Decorate with mint sprigs.

Baked Grapefruit with Ginger*

FOR 4

2 fresh grapefruit; preserved ginger; 4 level teaspoons soft brown sugar

Preparation: 5 minutes *Cooking time: about 15 minutes*

If you are not ginger addicts leave out the ginger and increase the sugar to heaped teaspoonfuls.

Cut the grapefruit in half. Divide into segments, removing as much of the membrane as possible. Pour 1 tablespoon of the ginger syrup over each grapefruit half, sprinkle with sugar and arrange thin slices of ginger round the edge. Fill the centre cavity with small pieces of ginger. Heat in slow oven for 10–15 minutes until the sugar has dissolved.

PÂTÉS

Country Pâté*

FOR THE GRAND OCCASION

FOR 12–15

3 bay leaves; 4 rashers streaky bacon, rinded; 8 oz. bread without crusts; 2 eggs; ¼ pint port or other fortified wine; 2 cloves garlic; ½ lb. belly pork; ½ lb. smoked bacon trimmings; 1 lb. pigs' liver; 1 lb. chicken livers; ½ teaspoon dried thyme; ½ teaspoon mixed herbs; 1 teaspoon ground mace or nutmeg; 3 level teaspoons salt; ½ level teaspoon freshly ground black pepper

Preparation: 20 minutes *Cooking time: about 2½ hours*

A really roughly textured liver pâté reminiscent of the country pâté that France is renowned for. When keeping the pâté in the refrigerator wrap in foil or plastic wrap as the aroma is deliciously potent and would easily flavour sweet foods or butter. This pâté is vast—plenty for 12 as a starter with some over too.

Get out a 3-pint terrine or loaf tin.

Set the oven at 325°F., Gas 3.

Well grease the terrine or loaf tin, arrange the 3 bay leaves in the centre of the base and cover neatly with streaky bacon rashers flattened and stretched with the blade of a knife on a board.

Soak bread in well beaten egg. Add port and mash well with a fork so that no large lumps remain. Finely chop or crush garlic, cut belly pork into strips then pass through a mincer with the bacon trimmings and liver.

Add the garlic, thyme, mixed herbs, mace and seasoning (if the bacon trimmings are salt add less salt) to the minced mixture. Finally stir in the bread mixture. Blend well together and turn into the prepared terrine or tin.

Cover with kitchen foil and lid, stand terrine in a large baking tin or dish of hot water, on a wire rack or crumpled foil to prevent the bottom of the pâté from over-baking. Bake at 325°F., Gas 3 for 2½ hours. If making half the amount it will take 2 hours to cook. Allow to cool, turn out and serve with toast and butter.

Pâté*

(Made in 5 minutes in the blender)

FOR 6–8

6 rashers streaky bacon, de-rinded; 1 egg; 4 slices white bread without crusts (4 oz.); 4 tablespoons port or madeira or, if these are not available, sherry; ½ lb. chicken livers; 1 clove garlic, peeled; ½ lb. pigs' liver; 2 level teaspoons salt; ⅛ level teaspoon freshly ground black pepper; ½ level teaspoon ground nutmeg; ¼ level teaspoon dried mixed herbs; ½ level teaspoon dried marjoram; 4 oz. bacon trimmings, cut in small pieces; 4 oz. lard, melted

Preparation: 10 minutes *Cooking time: about 2½ hours*

Get out a 2½-pint loaf tin or deep pie dish.

Set oven at 325°F., Gas 3.

Stretch the 6 rashers of streaky bacon with the back of a knife on a board, then use them to line the base and sides of the tin or dish. Put the egg into the blender with the bread, broken in small pieces, and the port and chicken livers. Reduce the mixture to a pulp in the blender, then pour it into a bowl. Put the garlic, pigs' liver, salt, pepper, spices, herbs and bacon trimmings into the blender and reduce these to a pulp. Mix the second mixture with the first in the bowl and stir in the melted lard. Pour the pâté into the lined tin or dish, cover it tightly with a lid of foil, place the tin in a meat tin containing ½ in. warm water and bake the pâté for about 2½ hours. Remove it from the oven and turn it out of the tin when it is cold.

FISH STARTERS

Buckling Pâté*

FOR 4–6

1 large buckling; 4 oz. softened butter; 1 tablespoon lemon juice or 2 tablespoons dry white wine; 1 crushed clove of garlic; freshly ground pepper

Preparation: 15 minutes

This is such an easy pâté to make. A buckling is a herring smoked at a high temperature for a long time, hence the mellow flavour. It is very similar to smoked trout but a good deal cheaper.

Skin and bone the buckling. The buckling is easier to skin and bone if it is first dropped into boiling water for one minute. Pound the flesh with a wooden spoon and blend together with the softened butter. Add the crushed clove of garlic and lemon juice. If you have a blender it will make the pâté in a few minutes. Put the buckling flesh, the butter—this should be softened under the grill until really soft, but not oily—crushed clove of garlic and lemon juice all in the blender and mix until smooth. Season to taste with pepper.

Turn into a small shallow stoneware jar or oval dish and fork a pattern over the top. Cover and keep in the refrigerator until required. Serve at room temperature so that it spreads easily with hot brown toast and plenty of butter.

Salade Niçoise*

FOR 4

3 tomatoes, skinned, quartered and pipped; ½ cucumber, peeled and diced; ½ lb. French beans, cooked and cut into 1½-inch lengths; 1 small green pepper, quartered, pipped and thinly sliced; 1 small onion, finely chopped; 1 clove garlic, crushed; 8 tablespoons French dressing; 1 cos lettuce, cut in 2-in. strips; 6-oz. can tuna, drained; 1 can anchovy fillets; 2 oz. black olives; 2 hard-boiled eggs

Preparation 15 minutes

This can be served on individual dishes or in one large bowl.

Prepare the tomatoes, cucumber, beans, pepper, onion, garlic and French dressing. Arrange the washed lettuce leaves in the bottom of a salad bowl or serving dish then add the garlic to the French dressing, followed by the prepared ingredients, anchovies and olives. Mix them thoroughly, then place them on top of the lettuce. Put the pieces of flaked tuna on top. Cut the hard-boiled eggs in half lengthwise and put these on top of the salad.

Scampi Provençal*

FOR THE GRAND OCCASION

FOR 4

1 oz. butter; 1 small onion, chopped; 1 clove garlic, crushed; 1 lb. tomatoes, skinned, quartered and pipped; 1 teaspoon chopped parsley; 1 teaspoon chopped chives; ½ lb. shelled scampi, cooked; 1 tablespoon dry sherry; salt and pepper

Preparation: 10 minutes *Cooking time: about 20 minutes*

Melt the butter in a pan. Add the onion and cook until soft but not coloured. Stir in the garlic, tomatoes, parsley and chives and simmer until the tomatoes are soft but still retain some of their shape. Stir in the sherry, scampi and seasoning. Reheat to boiling point and serve with plain boiled rice or brown bread and butter.

Prawn Vol-au-Vents

FOR 6

Six 3-in. frozen or cooked vol-au-vent cases or, to make your own, 11-oz. packet frozen puff pastry; egg glaze

For filling: 1 oz. butter; 1 oz. flour; ½ pint milk; 4–6 oz. shelled prawns or shrimps; salt and pepper; anchovy essence; chopped parsley

Preparation: 15 minutes *Total cooking time: about 35 minutes*

Set oven at 400°F., Gas 6.

Allow the pastry to defrost at room temperature, then roll out ¼ in. thick on a well-floured board. Cut into 6 ovals or circles with a pastry cutter. Make a smaller cut a ¼ in. inside each case but do not cut completely through the pastry. Place on an ungreased baking sheet and, if possible, leave in the refrigerator for half an hour to chill. Brush the tops of the cases with egg glaze or milk. Bake at 400°F., Gas 6 for 20 minutes or until well risen and golden brown.

Remove from the baking sheet and cool on a wire rack. Carefully remove the 'lids' with a sharp knife and scoop out any uncooked mixture.

Prepare the filling: melt the butter in a small pan, blend in the flour and cook for 1 minute. Stir in the milk a little at a time. Bring to the boil and simmer until thickened. Season well with salt and pepper. Add anchovy essence and the chopped parsley. Stir in the prawns. Taste and add more anchovy essence and seasoning if needed. Fill the prepared cases with the mixture, replace the lids. Before serving reheat at 400°F., Gas 6 for 10–15 minutes.

Coquilles St. Jacques*

FOR THE GRAND OCCASION

FOR 6

6 scallops; 1 oz. butter; 1 shallot, peeled and chopped; 1 stick celery, chopped; 1 sprig thyme; 1 bay leaf; ½ pint dry white wine; salt; pepper

For the sauce: 1 oz. butter; 1 oz. flour; ½ pint cooking liquor from the scallops

1 lb. potatoes, peeled, cooked and mashed; ½ oz. butter; milk; salt; pepper

Preparation: 20 minutes *Total cooking time: about 30 minutes*

Get ready 6 scallop shells.

First cook the scallops. Melt the butter in a pan and fry the shallot with the celery, thyme and bay leaf until the shallot is soft but not coloured. Add the wine and simmer for 2 minutes. Season with salt and pepper, add the scallops and simmer them gently for 5 minutes. Remove the scallops from the pan and strain the liquor into a measuring jug.

Meanwhile add enough milk with the butter to the mashed potato to give a soft piping consistency. Season the potato with salt and pepper, then put it into a large piping bag containing a large rose pipe and decorate the edge of each scallop shell with potato, then brown the potato under the grill.

Make a white sauce with the butter, flour and the cooking liquor from the scallops. Bring it to boiling point and simmer it until the sauce is thick and smooth. Season it with salt and pepper. Add the scallops cut in 1-in. pieces and reheat them for 1 minute. Divide the scallops and sauce between the six shells and serve piping hot. These may be made 12 hours or so in advance, put in the refrigerator, then reheated at 400°F., Gas 6 for 15 minutes.

Moules Marinière

FOR 4–6

6 pints fresh mussels; 1 oz. butter; 4 shallots, peeled and chopped; 4 parsley stalks; 2 sprigs fresh thyme or ¼ level teaspoon dried thyme; 1 bay leaf; freshly ground black pepper; ½ pint dry white wine; salt; chopped parsley

For the beurre manié: 1 oz. butter, creamed and softened; ½ oz. flour

Preparation: 15 minutes *Cooking time: about 35 minutes*

Scrape and clean each mussel with a strong knife, removing every trace of seaweed, mud and beard. Wash in several changes of water, discarding any which are badly chipped or cracked or ones that do not close tightly. Mussels which remain open are dead and should not be used. Drain the mussels in a colander.

Melt the butter in a large pan over a low heat. Fry the shallots until they are soft but not coloured. Add the herbs, pepper and wine, and then the mussels. Cover the pan with a tightly fitting lid and cook quickly, shaking the pan constantly, until the mussels open—about 5 to 6 minutes. Lift the mussels out of the pan, discard the empty half of each shell, and keep hot in a covered serving dish. Reduce the cooking liquor to about half a pint. Remove the fresh thyme, parsley stalks and bay leaf.

Blend the flour and butter for the beurre manié to a smooth paste. Drop the beurre manié into the simmering stock a teaspoon at a time and whisk it until the stock is smooth and has thickened. Add more pepper and salt if necessary. Pour the stock over the mussels and scatter with plenty of chopped parsley.

Serve with French bread and butter. Finger bowls are a help, as picking up mussels is a messy process. You need a dish for the empty shells.

MAYONNAISE AND FRENCH DRESSING

Home-made mayonnaise is one of the sauces that many seem rather terrified of tackling because of the fear of its curdling. This is caused either through the egg yolks and oil not being at the same room temperature or through adding the oil too quickly to the egg yolks and not therefore giving it time to be well beaten in and allowed to emulsify with the yolk mixture. In France this emulsifying is done with a lot of elbow grease and a wooden spoon. I find it best to use a small wire hand or machine rotary whisk as this creates more movement with less effort! Naturally, an electric mixer allows the oil to be added a little more quickly as it may be poured very slowly from a jug until it has all been included. Once made, the mayonnaise will keep for a month in an airtight plastic container or jar in the refrigerator.

Mayonnaise*

2 egg yolks; ½ level teaspoon made mustard; ½ level teaspoon salt; ⅛ level teaspoon pepper; ½ level teaspoon caster sugar; ½ pint olive, vegetable or corn oil; 1 tablespoon lemon juice; 1 tablespoon white wine vinegar or cider vinegar

Preparation: 10 minutes

Stand a bowl on a damp cloth to prevent it slipping on the table. Put in the egg yolks, mustard, salt, pepper and sugar; mix thoroughly then add the oil drop by drop, beating well with a whisk the whole time until the sauce is thick and smooth (in order that the oil may be added a drop at a time put into the bottle neck a cork from which a small wedge has been cut). Beat in the vinegar and lemon juice—this makes a thick, traditional mayonnaise.

Add a little cream or top of the milk for a thinner mixture. Should the sauce curdle through adding the oil too quickly to the egg yolks take a fresh egg yolk and begin again, adding the curdled mayonnaise very slowly in the same way as the oil is added to the original egg yolks.

Prawn or Shrimp Cocktail Sauce*

¼ pint home-made mayonnaise; 1 level teaspoon tomato purée; ¼ level teaspoon caster sugar; few drops Worcestershire sauce; few drops chilli sauce; 1 tablespoon lemon juice; 2 tablespoons double cream; freshly ground black pepper

Preparation: 5 minutes

Mix all the ingredients together and season well with black pepper.

French Dressing*

½ clove garlic, crushed; ½ level teaspoon dry mustard; about ½ level teaspoon salt; ⅛ level teaspoon freshly ground black pepper; 1 level teaspoon very finely chopped onion or a few finely chopped chives or onion tops; 1 level teaspoon caster sugar; ¼ pint olive, vegetable or corn oil; 4–6 tablespoons of preferably white wine vinegar (or half white wine vinegar and half distilled malt vinegar or lemon juice)

Preparation: 10 minutes

Blend the first six ingredients together in a bowl. Mix in the oil slowly with a whisk or spoon. Finally stir in the vinegars or vinegar and lemon juice. Taste and adjust the seasoning if necessary.

For a simpler French dressing that will keep omit the garlic, chives or onion and lemon juice if used. Put all the ingredients together in a screw-top jar, replace the lid and shake vigorously until well blended. In this way the ingredients can be proportionately increased and more made at one time. The dressing can be kept in the jar in a cool place for up to six weeks to be used as required. A variety of ingredients may then be added.

THE CENTRE ATTRACTION

ROASTED TO A TURN

When roasting a joint it is important to consider the cut of meat. The cheaper cuts of roasting meat should certainly be roasted slowly. If the meat has been frozen, thaw it slowly in the refrigerator before cooking to get the best results.

Stand the joint on a trivet or rack in the roasting tin while it is roasting. Put one tablespoon of fat or dripping in the meat tin. Before roasting brush the joint over with oil or rub with a butter paper. Sprinkle with salt and pepper. Baste the meat with fat from time to time during cooking.

Before roasting weigh the meat, including any stuffing, of course, then calculate the cooking time from the roasting chart below. If covering with foil for part of the cooking time remember either to increase the oven temperature or to cook for a little longer.

ROASTING TIMES

Beef

Oven Roast	*Slow Roast*
400°F., Gas 6	325°F., Gas 3
FOR SMALLER JOINTS	FOR SMALLER JOINTS
15 mins. per lb. plus 15 mins.	30 mins. per lb. plus 20 mins.
FOR THICKER JOINTS	FOR THICKER JOINTS
20 mins. per lb. plus 20 mins.	35 mins. per lb. plus 25 mins.

FOR LARGER, BONED JOINTS
25 mins. per lb. plus 25 mins.

FOR LARGER, BONED JOINTS
40 mins. per lb. plus 30 mins.

Serve with: Yorkshire pudding; made mustard and horseradish sauce; thin gravy.

Veal

Oven Roast
400°F., Gas 6

FOR JOINTS WITH A BONE
25 mins. per lb. plus 25 mins.

FOR BONED JOINTS
30 mins. per lb. plus 30 mins.

Slow Roast
325°F., Gas 3

FOR JOINTS WITH A BONE
50 mins per lb. plus 50 mins.

Veal is best covered whilst roasting. Remove the cover for the last half-hour so that the meat can brown.
Serve with: well flavoured gravy; parsley and thyme stuffing, page 72.

Pork

Oven Roast
425°F., Gas 7 for 20 mins.—
to crisp crackling
400°F., Gas 6 for the remaining
cooking time

FOR JOINTS WITH BONE
30 mins. per lb. plus 30 mins.

FOR BONED JOINTS
35 mins. per lb. plus 35 mins.

Slow Roast
Not suitable

To prepare the joint: have your butcher score the fat deeply. For really crisp crackling rub the scored fat with dry mustard, brush liberally with oil or fat and sprinkle with salt.
Serve with: apple sauce, page 71; sage and onion stuffing, page 71; thickened gravy, page 70.

Lamb

Oven Roast	*Slow Roast*
400°F., Gas 6	325°F., Gas 3
FOR SMALL OR THIN JOINTS, e.g. SHOULDER 20 mins per lb. plus 20 mins.	FOR SMALL OR THIN JOINTS 30 mins. per lb. plus 30 mins.
FOR THICKER JOINTS 25 mins. per lb. plus 25 mins.	FOR THICKER JOINTS 35 mins. per lb. plus 35 mins.
FOR BONED, LARGER JOINTS 30 mins. per lb. plus 30 mins.	FOR BONED, LARGER JOINTS 45 mins. per lb. plus 45 mins.

Serve with: mint sauce, page 70 or red currant jelly and thin gravy, page 70

Chicken

Oven Roast	*Slow Roast*
400°F., Gas 6 for 15 mins. per lb.	325°F., Gas 3 for 20–22 mins. per lb.
Baste occasionally	Baste occasionally

Serve with: bacon rolls; small chipolata sausages; bread sauce, page 215; thin brown gravy, page 70; watercress; also stuffing, if liked.

To prepare the chicken: allow the chicken to thaw completely if it is frozen. Fill the centre cavity with stuffing or put a sprig of herbs and a large knob of butter inside. Smear with a little butter and cover the breast with bacon rashers.

Duck

Oven Roast	*Slow Roast*
400°F., Gas 6 for 15 mins. per lb.	325°F., Gas 3 for 20 mins. per lb.

Serve with: watercress; peas; apple sauce; thin gravy; orange salad.

To prepare the duck: stuff the duck with sage and onion stuffing at the tail end. A duckling does not need stuffing. Sprinkle the breast with salt and pepper.

Goose

Oven Roast	*Slow Roast*
400°F., Gas 6 for 15 mins. per lb. plus 15 mins.	350°F., Gas 4 for 25 mins. to 30 mins. per lb.

Serve with: giblet gravy, page 70; gooseberry or apple sauce, page 71;

To prepare the goose: stuff with sage and onion stuffing or veal force-meat stuffing. Sprinkle the goose with salt and spread with a little fat. Baste frequently. Cover with buttered greaseproof paper till the last 30 minutes.

Turkey

Cook at 350°F., Gas 4 allowing 15 mins. per lb. plus 15 mins. for birds 15 lb. and under, 12 minutes per lb. plus 12 mins. if the bird is over 15 lb. Cover bird loosely with foil for the first part of cooking time; for last 30–40 minutes remove to allow browning.

Serve with: giblet gravy; chipolata sausages; bacon rolls; chestnut or lemon and thyme stuffing; cranberry sauce; bread sauce; watercress.

See pages 211–13

Pheasant

Pheasants are in season from 1 October to 1 February. After being shot the bird should hang in a cool, airy larder for about one week, depending on the weather and how high you like the pheasant to be. Pluck and draw it before cooking.

Place a piece of butter inside the bird and season the inside with salt, pepper and lemon juice. Truss the bird, cover the breast with bacon rashers and place it on a trivet inside a meat tin.

Roast at 425°F., Gas 7 for 10 minutes, then reduce the oven temperature to 400°F., Gas 6. Allow 30 to 40 minutes in all for a young bird and 40 to 60 minutes for an older bird. Baste it frequently. About 10 minutes before the end of the cooking time remove the bacon rashers from the breast, dredge the breast with flour and return the bird to the oven.

Serve with watercress, potato crisps, brown breadcrumbs, bread sauce, thin gravy. Cranberry sauce, red currant jelly, green salad, orange salad or stuffed oranges may also be served.

Grouse

Grouse are in season from 12 August to 10 December. Hang birds as for pheasant. Very young birds may be eaten after two days.

One bird will serve one to two portions according to size.

Pluck, draw and truss the bird. Put a knob of butter, seasoned with salt and pepper, inside the bird and place it on a slice of toast in a meat tin. Put a rasher of bacon over the breast. Roast the bird for 15 to 45 minutes according to age at 400°F., Gas 6.

Remove the bacon about 10 minutes before the end of the cooking time. Dredge the breast with flour and return the bird to the oven to brown. Serve it on the toast on which it has been cooked, garnished with watercress.

Serve with thin gravy, bread sauce, fried crumbs, potato crisps or straw potatoes.

CLASSIC ETCETERAS FOR ROASTS

Yorkshire Pudding

FOR 6

4 oz. plain flour; ¼ level teaspoon salt; 1 egg, beaten; about ½ pint milk and water (half milk and half water)

Preparation: 5 minutes *Cooking time: about 15–30 minutes*

Get out a shallow Yorkshire pudding tin or 12-hole deep bun tin.

Set the oven at 425°F., Gas 7.

Sift the flour and salt into a bowl. Make a well in the centre of the flour and blend in the egg with a little of the milk, using a small wire whisk to make a smooth paste. Blend in enough of the remaining milk to make a batter the consistency of double cream. Beat it well. Put a little fat or dripping into the bottom of the tin or tins and put the tin or tins into the oven to become hot. Remove them from the oven and pour in the batter. Cook a large pudding for about 30 minutes and small puddings for about 15 minutes until well risen and golden brown.

Serve at once.

Gravy

Remove the roast meat from the meat tin when it is cooked, then carefully pour away any fat so that only the sediment from the meat tin remains in the tin.

Thin gravy: Put about ½ pint of, preferably, stock (for birds use the giblet stock) or water from the vegetables into the meat tin and bring it to boiling point. Simmer it until it has reduced by half, scraping the sediment from the bottom of the tin as the stock is simmering. Add plenty of salt and pepper and a few drops of gravy browning if required.

Thick gravy: Leave one tablespoon of fat in the meat tin and blend in 1 or 2 level tablespoons flour, depending on how thick you like the finished gravy to be. Cook this roux over a low heat, stirring constantly and scraping the sediment from the bottom of the tin until the roux is light brown. Blend in about ½ pint stock or liquid from the vegetables, bring it to boiling point and simmer it for 2 or 3 minutes. Add gravy browning to give it a good colour and plenty of salt and pepper. Strain the gravy into a gravy boat and serve at once.

Mint Sauce

2 rounded tablespoons chopped mint; 2 teaspoons caster sugar; 1 tablespoon boiling water; 1 to 2 tablespoons vinegar

Preparation: 5 minutes

Wash and dry the mint well, then strip the leaves from the stem and chop them finely. Put the sugar into a sauce boat with the water and stir until the sugar has dissolved. Add the chopped mint and vinegar to taste. Add more sugar if liked.

Dienstag
Tuesday
Mardi

8

9

10

11

12

13

14

15

16

17

Montag
Monday
Lundi
KUKA
TIMER
8
9
10
11
12
13
14
15
16
17

Horseradish Cream

1 tablespoon grated horseradish; 2½-fl. oz. carton double cream, lightly whipped, or ½ small can sweetened condensed milk; salt; pepper; 1 tablespoon vinegar or lemon juice

Preparation: 5 minutes

Wash and scrape the horseradish and grate it into very fine flakes. Or use grated horseradish from a jar. Add it to the cream or condensed milk, stir in the seasoning and lastly the lemon juice or vinegar. Blend thoroughly and, if cream is used, add a dash of sugar. Chill before serving. Alternatively, use one of the prepared horseradish creams.

Apple Sauce

1 lb. cooking apples, peeled, cored and sliced; 3 tablespoons water; juice of ½ lemon; 1 oz. butter; sugar to taste

Preparation: 10 minutes

Put the apple slices into a pan with the water and lemon juice. Cover the pan and cook the apples until they are soft, then remove the lid and beat the apples with a wooden spoon until they are smooth. Add the butter, then sugar as liked.

Pour the sauce into a sauce boat and serve cold. If it is being served with goose, duck or pork the sauce should be fairly tart.

If you are in a hurry use canned apple purée.

Sage and Onion Stuffing

2 large onions; ½ to 1 oz. butter; 4 oz. fresh white breadcrumbs; 2 level teaspoons dried sage; 1 level teaspoon salt; ½ level teaspoon freshly ground black pepper

Preparation: 10 minutes

Peel the onions, put them into a pan of cold water, bring this to boiling point and simmer them for about 20 minutes until just tender. Drain well and chop, then add the butter, breadcrumbs, sage and seasonings, and mix well.

Use for stuffing goose and duck or pork.

Parsley and Thyme Stuffing

2 oz. suet, shredded; 4 oz. fresh white breadcrumbs; 2 tablespoons parsley, chopped; ½ level teaspoon dried mixed herbs; finely grated rind of 1 lemon; salt; pepper; beaten egg

Preparation: 10 minutes

Mix together the suet and breadcrumbs in a bowl. Add the parsley, herbs and lemon rind, season the mixture well with salt and pepper and add enough egg to bind it together.

Use for stuffing lamb, veal and chicken, also savoury forcemeat balls.

Roast Saddle of Lamb FOR THE GRAND OCCASION

FOR 6

Saddle of lamb, weight as required; 2 oz. good dripping; 2 sprigs rosemary; pepper; salt

Gravy: 2 tablespoons meat fat; 1 oz. flour; ½ pint stock; 1 teaspoon red currant jelly; pepper; salt; 2 tablespoons sherry

Preparation: 5 minutes

This is an expensive joint but well worth having for a special occasion.

Set oven at 375°F., Gas 5.

Ask your butcher to cut the weight of meat you would like for your guests. For six take a saddle of spring lamb which weighs between 4½–7 lb. or a half a full saddle of young mutton which can weigh up to 10 lb. This cut is the two loins together from ribs to tail. The kidneys are sometimes sent attached to the saddle and may be roasted and served with the joint, a slice being served with each portion, or they may be removed and used for another dish.

Your butcher may offer to decorate the fat of the meat for you, but if not, you can make the flowers very simply by scooping out the fat with a sharp knife to form petals and lifting them out of the fat. Cover each flower with a small piece of foil to protect them during cooking. This should be removed 20 minutes before the end to crisp the fat. Any other design may be scored on the side if liked.

Roast the joint, in a large meat tin, allowing 25 minutes to the pound and 25 minutes over. Before putting it in the oven (375°F., Gas 5) spread it with dripping, tuck the two sprigs of rosemary under the joint to give added flavour and sprinkle with pepper and salt. Start roasting the joint with a piece of foil or greaseproof paper over it. Remove after half an hour; this prevents excessive browning. Serve with gravy and mint sauce.

TO MAKE GRAVY: Strain off all but 2 tablespoons of the fat from the meat. To this add the flour and cook on top of the stove in the meat tin for a few minutes until the flour is golden brown, stirring briskly all the time with a wooden spoon. Remove from the heat and slowly add stock, return to the heat, bring to the boil and allow to thicken, stirring all the time. Add red currant jelly and seasonings with the sherry.

Roast Lamb Anna Style

FOR 6

2 lb. potatoes, peeled; 2 oz. dripping; 3 lb. leg of lamb; salt; pepper; 1 or 2 cloves garlic

Preparation: 10 minutes

The sliced potatoes baked with the roast leg of lamb have a delicious flavour.

Set oven at 400°F., Gas 6.

Cut the potatoes into ½-in. thick slices. Make a bed, with the potato slices overlapping slightly, in a heavy oven-proof dish or meat tin. Dot most of the dripping over the potatoes and season it with salt and pepper. Cut the garlic into small spiky pieces and insert the pieces in the fat of the lamb. Spread with the dripping that is left. Place the joint on top of the potatoes in the tin. Roast it at 400°F., Gas 6 for 25 minutes to the pound plus 25 minutes, basting it from time to time. Remove the joint from the oven, carve it and serve it with the potatoes.

Roast Stuffed Veal

FOR 6 AND SOME FOR SERVING COLD NEXT DAY

About 4 lb. piece boned shoulder of veal; 2 tablespoons lemon juice; salt; pepper; lard

Stuffing: 1 small lemon; ¼ lb. calves' or pigs' liver, finely chopped or minced; 1 small onion, peeled and finely chopped; ½ oz. butter; 1 lb. pork sausage meat; 4 oz. fresh white breadcrumbs; 1 egg; 1 level teaspoon dried thyme; 1 heaped tablespoon chopped parsley; 1 level teaspoon salt; ⅛ level teaspoon pepper

Preparation: 15 minutes

The liver, sausage and parsley stuffing makes the joint more interesting if you are having it cold the next day.

Set oven at 400°F., Gas 6.

TO MAKE STUFFING: Grate lemon rind. Sauté finely chopped liver and onion in butter for 2–3 minutes. Thoroughly mix sausage meat, breadcrumbs, lemon rind and egg and combine with chopped liver and onion mixture, add the herbs and seasoning.

Lay meat out on a board, splitting where necessary to flatten to an oblong shape. Spread with stuffing, having left 2 in. clean down one side to allow for spreading and rolling joint up. Roll tightly, securing with skewers, and tie neatly with string at ¾-in. intervals. Place on a square of foil in a meat tin, pour over the lemon juice, salt and pepper, spread with lard. Cook in the oven at 400°F., Gas 6, for 30 minutes per lb. plus 30 minutes. Remove foil and cook for a further 20 minutes until the top of the joint is crisp and golden. Serve with red currant jelly if liked and for a really delicious gravy add a sherry glass of port or red wine to the stock.

SIMMER TILL TENDER

This batch of casseroled dishes varies in degrees of simplicity. The three great pluses of casseroles are that they use the cheaper cuts of meat, that they improve with long slow cooking, and once in the oven need little looking after. It is well worth while to double up on the quantities for the grander dishes and enjoy more than one meal from the same pot.

Sadie's Casserole—Without Fuss*

FOR 4

1½ lb. stewing steak; 3 carrots, peeled; 3 onions, peeled; 1 small can tomato soup; the small can, when emptied, filled with water; 1 oz. flour; 1 gravy cube; salt; pepper; pinch mixed herbs

Preparation: 10 minutes — *Cooking time: about 4 hours*

This casserole takes 10 minutes to get in the oven and then just cooks itself.

Get out an oven-proof casserole.

Set oven at 325°F., Gas 3.

Cut the steak up into 1-in. pieces. Chop up the carrots and onions roughly. Put the meat and vegetables with the tomato soup into the casserole. Add the flour blended with the water, the gravy cube, plenty of seasoning and the herbs. Cover the casserole and cook it in the oven at 325°F., Gas 3 for about 3 to 4 hours, according to the cut of stewing steak used.

Boeuf Bourguignonne*

FOR THE GRAND OCCASION

FOR 4

1½ lb. chuck steak; 1 oz. lard or bacon fat; 6 oz. streaky bacon, de-rinded and cut in ½-in. wide strips; ½ oz. flour; ½ pint stock or ½ pint water and a beef stock cube; ¼ pint Spanish type Burgundy;

1 bay leaf; $\frac{1}{2}$ level teaspoon dried mixed herbs; sprig of parsley; about $\frac{1}{2}$ level teaspoon salt; $\frac{1}{8}$ level teaspoon pepper; $\frac{1}{4}$ lb. small, even-sized onions, peeled

Preparation: 20 minutes *Cooking time: about 2½ hours*

Get out a 3-pint oven-proof casserole.

Set oven at 325°F., Gas 3.

Cut the steak into 1½-in. squares. Melt the lard or bacon fat in a fairly large pan and fry the bacon for a few minutes until it begins to turn brown. Lift the bacon out of the pan and into the casserole and then fry the steak in the fat remaining in the pan until it is brown all over. Then add the steak to the bacon in the casserole and pour off all but 2 tablespoons of the fat. Blend the flour with the 2 tablespoons fat in the pan and continue to cook until it has browned. Remove the pan from the heat and stir in the stock and wine. Return the pan to the heat and bring the liquor to boiling point. Simmer until it has thickened, then add the bay leaf, herbs, parsley and seasoning, adding only a little of the salt as the bacon may be salty. Pour the liquor over the meat, cover the casserole and simmer gently in the oven for 1½ hours.

Then add the onions to the casserole and cook it for a further hour or until the meat is really tender. Check the seasoning and add more salt and pepper if necessary. Skim off any fat on the surface with a spoon or 'blot' the top with kitchen paper to absorb the excess fat.

Swiss Steak*

FOR 4

1½ lb. chuck steak, cut in a 1-in. thick slice; 1½ oz. flour; 1 level teaspoon salt; $\frac{1}{4}$ level teaspoon pepper; 1½ oz. lard; 3 onions, peeled and finely sliced; 2 sticks celery, finely sliced; 8-oz. can tomatoes; 2 level teaspoons tomato purée; $\frac{1}{2}$ teaspoon Worcestershire sauce; $\frac{1}{4}$ pint water

Preparation: 15 minutes *Cooking time: about 2½–3 hours*

Set oven at 300°F., Gas 2.

Cut the steak into 8 pieces. Mix together the flour, salt and pepper. Toss the meat in the flour mixture, pressing it in so that all the flour is used. Melt the lard in a pan, fry the meat quickly on all sides until brown. Transfer it to an oven-proof casserole. Add the onion and celery to the fat remaining in the pan and fry until pale golden brown. Add to the meat with the tomatoes, purée, Worcestershire sauce and water. Cover and cook at 300°F., Gas 2 for 2½ hours or until tender.

Steak in a Parcel

FOR 4

1½ pint packet leek soup mix; 1½ lb. chuck steak in one piece; ¼ pint water; 2 tablespoons sherry; 2 bay leaves

Preparation: 5 minutes *Cooking time: about 3–4 hours*

The leeks give a mild oniony flavour in this dish, which needs little preparation and cooks itself in a parcel of foil.

Set oven at 325°F., Gas 3.

Blend half the contents of the soup packet with the water and simmer in a pan until it has thickened. Put the remaining soup powder on one side for future use. Stir the sherry into the soup in the pan. Put the steak onto a large piece of foil and then place it in a small deep baking tin. Pour the soup over the steak, put the bay leaves on top and wrap the foil loosely round the steak to form a secure parcel. Put it in the pre-heated oven and cook for 3–4 hours or until the meat is tender.

Steak and Kidney Pudding*

FOR 4

For the filling: 1 lb. skirt beef stewing steak; ¼ lb. ox kidney; 1 oz. flour; salt; pepper; water

For the pastry: 8 oz. self-raising flour; ½ level teaspoon salt; 4 oz. shredded suet; about 8 tablespoons cold water

Preparation: 20 minutes *Cooking time: at least 4½ hours*

Good old-fashioned steak and kidney pud. A dish that has survived and flourished for centuries. My grandmother attributed her success with this dish to long slow cooking.

Get out a 2-pint capacity pudding basin.

Cut the steak into 1-in. cubes. Remove the skin, core and fat from the kidney and then cut it into ½-in. pieces. To save the washing up put the flour into a paper bag with plenty of salt and pepper, enough to season the meat well as it cannot be adjusted at the end. Then shake the steak in the bag until it is well coated with the flour.

Sift the flour and salt into a basin, then stir in the suet. Add enough of the water to make a fairly soft dough like a scone dough. If some flour is still left in the bowl add a little more water so that the bowl is almost clean. Roll out two-thirds of the pastry to form a circle large enough to line the base and sides of the pudding basin. Lift the pastry circle into the basin and press into shape, pulling it up to the top of the basin.

Roll out the remaining pastry to a circle the size of the top of the basin. Put the steak and kidney in alternate layers in the basin, then add sufficient water to come up to within one inch of the top of the basin. Moisten the edges of the pastry with water and press the pastry lid firmly on to it.

Grease a sheet of greaseproof paper. To allow room for the pudding to expand make a large pleat in the paper and use it to cover the top of the pudding, tucking the paper under to form a firm cover. Repeat the process with a sheet of foil, making sure that the pleat in the foil runs the same way as the pleat in the greaseproof paper. Put the pudding basin into the top of a steamer above boiling water or into a large pan filled with sufficient water to come within half an inch of the foil cover. Cover the pan and leave the pudding to steam or simmer for 4½ hours, topping up the saucepan with more boiling water as necessary. Do not let the pudding go off the boil.

Lancashire Hot Pot*

FOR 4

2 lb. middle neck of lamb; ½ oz. flour; salt; pepper; 1½ lb. potatoes, peeled and cut into ¼-in. thick slices; ½ lb. onions, peeled and sliced; 2 lamb's kidneys, skinned, cored and quartered; ¼ lb. button mushrooms, sliced; ¾ pint stock or ¾ pint water and a beef stock cube; ½ oz. lard or dripping

Preparation: 20 minutes *Cooking time: about 2¾ hours*

Just the thing for leaving in the oven to cook itself whilst you are out for the morning.

Get out a 2½–3-pint casserole.

Set oven at 350°F., Gas 4.

Cut the lamb into even-sized chops and pieces. Mix the flour with a little salt and pepper and toss the chops with the flour. Put the onions into the casserole and arrange the chops, kidneys and mushrooms on top. Put the potato slices on top of the meat and then pour on the stock. Cut the lard or dripping into small pieces and put this on top of the potatoes. Cover the dish with a lid or else a lid of foil, and bake the hot pot at 350°F., Gas 4 for about 2½ hours. About 20–30 minutes before serving remove the lid so that the potatoes can brown.

Boiled Mutton with Caper Sauce*

FOR 6–8 AND TO SERVE SLICED COLD FOR ANOTHER DAY

1 small leg or ½ large leg of mutton; 2 onions, peeled; 6 cloves; 2 carrots, peeled and diced; 3 sticks celery, diced; juice of ½ lemon; ¼ level teaspoon dried thyme; sprig of parsley; 6 peppercorns; blade of mace

For the sauce: 1 oz. butter; 1 oz. flour; ¾ pint broth from the mutton; 1 to 2 tablespoons capers; 1 teaspoon vinegar from the capers; ½ teaspoon made English mustard; salt; pepper; a good tablespoon of cream or top of the milk, if available, improves the sauce

Preparation: 20 minutes *Cooking time: 2–3½ hours according to size of joint.*

A traditional British recipe well worth remembering.

Put the meat into a large pan and cover it with water. Bring the water to boiling point and remove the scum as it forms. When no more scum is forming add the onions, stuck with the cloves, the carrots, celery, lemon juice, thyme, parsley, peppercorns and mace to the pan. Cover with a lid and simmer the meat gently, allowing 25 minutes per pound.

If the meat is to be used next day allow it to cool in its own liquor then skim off the fat.

Prepare the sauce. Melt the butter in a pan, blend in the flour and cook for 1 minute over a low heat. Remove the pan from the heat and stir in the cooking liquor a little at a time, mixing well. Return the pan to the heat and simmer the sauce until it has thickened, stirring all the time. Add the capers, vinegar, mustard, seasoning and cream if used.

Osso Buco*

FOR THE GRAND OCCASION

FOR 4

2 to 2½ lb. knuckle veal or, if not available, 1½ lb. pie veal or boneless shin of veal; 3 carrots, peeled and thinly sliced; 2 sticks of celery, sliced; 1 onion, peeled and chopped; 1 tablespoon salad oil; ½ oz. butter; ½ oz. flour; ¼ pint white Chianti or dry white wine; 1 clove garlic, crushed; ½ pint white stock or ½ pint water and a chicken stock cube; 15-oz. can tomatoes; 1 sprig parsley; 1 bay leaf; salt; pepper

For the garnish: grated rind of ½ lemon; 2 tablespoons coarsely chopped parsley; ½ clove garlic, crushed

Preparation: 30 minutes *Cooking time: 2½–3½ hours*

Set oven at 325°F., Gas 3.

A rich Italian stew traditionally made from knuckle of veal, carefully preserving the entirety of the marrow in the bone. (If you have difficulty in getting knuckle you can make this stew with shin or pie veal instead.) It is traditional to serve Risotto alla Milanese with Osso Buco.

Ask your butcher to saw the knuckle into 1½- to 2-in. convenient-sized chunks. If using pie veal it is bought already cut up but if using shin cut it into 1½-in. pieces. Prepare the vegetables and set them on one side. Heat the oil in a heavy frying pan, add the butter and fry half the meat at a time over a moderate heat, turning it once, until the meat is golden brown. Take care not to let the marrow slip out of the knuckle bone.

Put the fried meat on to a piece of absorbent kitchen paper to drain, then lift it into the casserole. Fry the vegetables lightly for 5 minutes.

FOR THE SAUCE: Sprinkle the flour on to the vegetables and continue to cook, stirring occasionally, until the flour is browned, then blend in the wine, garlic, stock, tomatoes, sprig of parsley, bay leaf, salt and pepper. Bring the mixture to boiling point.

Pour the sauce on to the meat. Cover the casserole with a lid, put it into the oven and cook it until tender. Meat from a young calf will take about 2½ hours, but an older animal will take longer.

Meanwhile prepare the garnish by mixing together the lemon rind, parsley and garlic. When the Osso Buco is cooked, remove it from the oven and either sprinkle it with the garnish just before serving or put the lemon rind, etc. in a small bowl for people to help themselves. This is the authentic garnish, but for non-purists the garlic may easily be left out.

Serve with Risotto alla Milanese.

Risotto Alla Milanese

FOR 4

2 oz. butter; 1 small onion, peeled and finely chopped; 8 oz. refined long-grain rice; ¼ pint dry white wine or Chianti; 1 pint chicken stock or 1 pint water and a chicken stock cube; salt; pepper; good pinch powdered saffron; 2 teaspoons water; 1 oz. Parmesan cheese, grated

Preparation: 15 minutes *Cooking time: about 35 minutes*

This is the classic accompaniment to serve with Osso Buco. The Risotto is bright yellow, being flavoured with saffron.

Melt 1 oz. of the butter in a pan and fry the onion over a low heat until it is soft but not coloured. Add the rice to the pan and continue to cook it for about 2 minutes. Pour on the wine and simmer it until it has reduced by half, then add the stock and plenty of salt and pepper. Bring the liquid to boiling point, cover the pan with a lid and simmer the risotto for about 20 minutes or until the rice is just tender and the liquid has been absorbed. Blend the saffron with the water and stir it into the rice, using a fork. Finally stir in the remaining butter, Parmesan and more seasoning if required. Turn the risotto into a serving dish and serve it at once.

Boiled Bacon with Sweet and Sour Sauce*

FOR 4–6

2 lb. boned and rolled end forehock of bacon

For the sauce: 1 tablespoon salad oil; 1 oz. butter; ¼ lb. onions, peeled and chopped; 2 level tablespoons tomato purée; 4 tablespoons distilled malt vinegar; 2 oz. soft brown sugar; 2 teaspoons Worcestershire sauce; 1 level teaspoon made mustard; few drops of chilli sauce; salt

Preparation: 15 minutes *Cooking time: just over an hour*

Cover the bacon joint with cold water and leave it to soak overnight. Next day put it into a large saucepan with fresh cold water and bring it slowly to boiling point, removing any scum as it forms.

Simmer the joint, covered, for 20 minutes per lb. plus an extra 20 minutes. When the bacon is cooked remove it from the pan and carefully peel off the rind. Cut the bacon in slices and coat with the sauce just before serving.

To prepare the sauce, heat the oil in a pan, add the butter and fry the onion until it is soft and pale golden brown. Blend in all the other ingredients, cover the pan and simmer the sauce for 10 minutes.

Jugged Hare* FOR THE GRAND OCCASION

FOR 6–10

1 hare, cut into neat pieces; 2 oz. bacon fat; 2 large peeled onions, each stuck with two cloves; 6 peppercorns; rind of ½ lemon; 1 stick celery, cut in 1-in. pieces; pinch cayenne pepper; bouquet garni (sprig of thyme, a bay leaf and 2 sprigs parsley tied together with string); 1 blade of mace; salt; pepper; about 2 pints water

For the liaison: 2½ oz. butter; 2 oz. flour

To add to the gravy: ¼ pint port; 1 tablespoon red currant jelly; the blood of the hare

To garnish: Forcemeat balls; chopped parsley

Preparation: 40 minutes *Cooking time: 2–3½ hours depending on the age of the hare*

Set oven at 325°F., Gas 3.

A classic British dish, perhaps more popular in our grandmothers' time than it is now — goodness knows why, because it is surprisingly cheap and not difficult to make. It is really only a glorified stew enriched with port and thickened with a liaison — butter kneaded with flour — to give a really smooth sauce, and the blood of the hare.

Take care not to overcook the hare but simmer it slowly. A leveret (young hare) will take about two hours and serve six, whereas an older hare will take over three hours and be enough for eight to ten. Jugged hare reheats well. The season for hares is from 1 August to 28 February. If you are given an undrawn hare it should be hung head downwards for a week to ten days according to the weather. Serve it with forcemeat balls, croûtons of fried bread and red currant jelly.

Divide the hare into neat joints, saving as much of the blood as possible. Your butcher will do this for you and more often than not will put it in a tin for you to carry home. Melt the bacon fat in a large frying pan and fry the joints briskly until they are a good brown colour.

Pack the joints into a large, heavy oven-proof casserole with the vegetables, spices, lemon rind, herbs, salt and pepper. Pour over the water and cover the casserole with a tightly fitting lid. Put it in the oven at 325°F., Gas 3 for about 2 3½ hours or until the hare is tender. Pour the gravy through a strainer into a pan and remove the vegetables, spices, lemon rind and herbs from the casserole.

To make the kneaded butter liaison, work the butter on a plate with a palette knife until it is soft, then knead in the flour a little at a time to form a smooth paste. Add the kneaded butter in small pieces to the gravy, whisking it until it is smooth. When all the kneaded butter has been added bring the gravy to boiling point and simmer it until it has thickened, stirring all the time. (Thickening the liquid in this way gives a smoother result than does the usual blending method.)

Add the port and red currant jelly to the gravy and simmer it gently until the jelly has dissolved. Blend two or three tablespoons of the gravy with the blood then add the blood to the rest of the gravy. The gravy must not be boiled after this stage or it will curdle. Adjust the seasoning with more salt and pepper.

Strain the gravy over the hare and garnish the hare with forcemeat balls and chopped parsley. Serve with red currant jelly.

Forcemeat Balls

MAKES 12 BALLS

1 oz. butter; 1 small onion, peeled and chopped; 2 rashers streaky bacon, de-rinded and chopped; 3 oz. fresh white breadcrumbs; grated rind of ½ lemon; 1 oz. suet, shredded; ¼ level teaspoon dried thyme; 1 tablespoon chopped parsley; salt and pepper; beaten egg; dried browned breadcrumbs

Melt the butter in a pan and cook the onion until it is soft but not coloured. Add the bacon and cook for about 2 minutes. Remove the pan from the heat and stir in the fresh breadcrumbs, lemon rind, suet, thyme, parsley, seasoning and enough beaten egg to bind the mixture together.

Roll the forcemeat into 12 small balls then coat them with beaten egg, followed by dried breadcrumbs. Fry the forcemeat balls in deep, hot fat or oil for about 5 minutes or until they are golden brown. Drain them on kitchen paper.

CREAM MAKES THE DIFFERENCE

When cream is added to stews and sauces it should be at the last minute. Take care not to boil it because if the sauce contains acid as most do (e.g. wine, vinegar, lemon juice, tomatoes, onions) it will curdle. Cream may safely be boiled on its own or with added non-acid flavouring. If you are preparing a casserole or something like Boeuf Stroganoff in advance, re-heat on the day and just before going to table stir in the cream.

Soured cream is ideal for such dishes as Boeuf Stroganoff and a product relatively new to this country although it has been used in continental cookery for years. It is not cream that has gone off. It smells fresh and tastes sharp and refreshing. When you open a carton, soured cream looks like set plain yoghurt, but is creamier. The consistency of soured cream is rather like lightly whipped double cream.

Soured cream is considerably cheaper than double cream because it contains less butter fat.

Boeuf Stroganoff

FOR THE GRAND OCCASION

FOR 4

1½ lb. fillet or rump steak; 2½ oz. butter; 1 large onion, peeled and chopped; 4 oz. button mushrooms, sliced; 2 tomatoes, skinned, pipped and chopped; 1 tablespoon salad oil; 2×5-oz. cartons soured cream or, if you can't get it, double cream soured with 1 tablespoon lemon juice; salt; pepper; watercress

Preparation: 15 minutes — *Cooking time: about 15 minutes*

Cut the steak into strips about 2 in. long, ½ in. wide and ¼ in. thick. Melt 1 oz. of the butter in a frying-pan and fry the onion slowly until it is soft. Remove the onion from the pan on to a plate and add another ½ oz. butter to the pan. Cook the mushrooms for 2 minutes then add the prepared tomato and cook for a further 2 minutes. Remove the mushroom and tomato mixture from the pan and add it to the onion. Melt the remaining butter in the pan with the oil and fry half the steak for about 4 minutes until it is just cooked. Remove the steak from the pan then fry the remaining steak in the same way.

Drain as much fat as possible from the pan then put all the steak, onion, mushrooms and tomato into the pan. Heat until piping hot. Season it well with salt and pepper then add the soured cream just before serving. Blend well and pour it into a serving dish and garnish it with watercress.

Veal Chops Provençal* FOR THE GRAND OCCASION

FOR 4

2 oz. butter; 1 tablespoon salad oil; 4 veal loin chops or 4 slices of fillet of veal

For the Provençal vegetable mixture: 2 large green peppers; 2 medium onions, peeled and quartered; 2 oz. butter; 2 small aubergines; ½ lb. tomatoes; ¼ pint white wine; ¼ pint single cream; salt; pepper

For garnish: Sprigs of watercress

Preparation: 20 minutes *Cooking time: about 40 minutes*

Melt the 2 oz. butter with the oil in the frying-pan and fry the veal chops fairly rapidly on both sides until they are golden brown, then reduce the heat and continue to cook them until they are tender, about 30 minutes in all, depending on the thickness of the chops.

Meanwhile prepare the Provençal vegetable mixture. Cut the peppers in half, remove the seeds and cut the flesh into ½-in. wide strips. Shred the onions coarsely. Melt the butter in the pan and fry the pepper and onion for about 5 minutes or until they are soft and the onion is pale golden brown. Remove the stalks from the aubergines and cut them into ¼-in. thick slices. Plunge the tomatoes into boiling water for 10 seconds then remove them from the water and peel off the skins. Quarter the tomatoes and remove the seeds. Add the aubergines and tomatoes to the contents of the saucepan and continue to cook for a further 5 minutes.

Remove the veal chops from the frying pan, arrange them on a serving dish and keep them hot. Add the wine to the fat and sediment in the frying pan, bring it to boiling point and simmer for 2 minutes or so, to reduce it by half. Add this to the vegetables in the pan, re-heat until piping hot. Add salt and pepper to taste. Just before serving stir in the cream, turn the vegetable mixture into a serving dish, arrange the veal chops on top, garnish with watercress and serve at once.

Porc Hongroise*

FOR 4

1½ lb. pork fillet; 2 tablespoons salad oil; 1 oz. butter; 1 onion, peeled and chopped; 1 level tablespoon paprika pepper; 1 level tablespoon flour; ½ pint stock or ½ pint water and a beef stock cube; 5 tablespoons sherry; 1 level teaspoon tomato purée; 6 oz. small button mushrooms; 1 level tablespoon cornflour and 2 tablespoons cold water, blended together; 2½-oz. carton double cream; salt; pepper

Preparation: 15 minutes *Cooking time: about 30 minutes*

A rich goulash using fillet of pork, which is all tender lean meat.

Cut the fillet into 1½-in. pieces. Heat the oil in a pan, add the butter and then fry the pieces of pork quickly on both sides until they are just beginning to turn brown. Remove them from the pan and drain them on absorbent kitchen paper. Fry the onion in the pan with the paprika for 2 minutes then blend in the flour and cook for a further minute. Remove the pan from the heat and blend in the stock. Add the sherry and tomato purée, return it to the heat and simmer until the sauce has thickened. Season with salt and pepper to taste, return the meat to the pan, cover and simmer for 15 minutes, or until cooked through.

At the end of the cooking time add the whole mushrooms to the pan together with the cornflour, which has been blended to a smooth paste with the water. Re-boil, adjust seasoning, simmer for 3 or 4 minutes and, just before serving, stir in the cream.

Lobster Newburg FOR THE GRAND OCCASION

FOR 2

$1\frac{1}{4}$–$1\frac{1}{2}$-lb. lobster or 2 × 1-lb. lobsters, cooked; $1\frac{1}{2}$ oz. butter; $\frac{1}{8}$ pint (5 tablespoons) medium dry sherry; $\frac{1}{4}$ pint double cream; 2 egg yolks; salt; pepper; cayenne

Preparation: 15 minutes *Cooking time: about 10–15 minutes*

This classic lobster dish is best cooked just before serving and is best served just with a tossed green salad.

Ask your fishmonger to split the lobsters and crack the claws. Remove the meat from the claws with a sharp knife. Melt the butter in a shallow pan, add the lobster flesh cut in pieces and cook gently for 4 minutes, turning once. Stir in the sherry and simmer until reduced to about 2 tablespoons. Stir in the cream, retaining about 2 tablespoons. Bring to just below boiling point. Mix the remaining cream with the egg yolks and add to the lobster mixture. Re-heat until slightly thickened but do not allow to boil at all.

Season with salt and pepper. Pile the mixture back into the lobster shells and sprinkle with cayenne pepper. Garnish with parsley.

TAKE A CHICKEN

Chickens are not quite the birds they used to be. It is hard to come by a fresh, free-range chicken full of flavour that has spent its life down on the farm enjoying plenty of green stuff as well as grain and pellets.

Most of the chickens in the shops are young birds, about 9–10 weeks old, that have been intensively farmed and are sold as broilers; they usually weigh about 2½–3 lb. Broiler chickens are comparatively cheap and if treated very carefully – take care not to overcook – they will make good chicken dishes. If roasting these birds try the French way with butter and a little stock. Real boiling fowls seem hard to come by; even these are younger than they used to be for it is an uneconomical proposition for a farmer to keep a hen past her laying peak. When possible use for casseroling. Remember that they may take time to cook – for the best flavour simmer slowly until tender; this will take at least 2½ hours. If it is rather a fatty bird remove excess fat from the bird first then simmer in the usual way till tender. Allow it to get cold in its own stock overnight then spoon off all the fat and re-heat. Make a sauce if the dish calls for one.

Chicken Casserole Post Haste!*

FOR 4

4 frying chicken joints; 10-oz. can condensed mushroom soup; 1 bay leaf; ⅛ pint single cream; salt; pepper; about 3 tablespoons sherry

Preparation: 10 minutes *Cooking time: about 2 hours*

Set oven at 325°F., Gas 3.

Just the thing if you are dashing out and want to leave a meal in the oven.

Put the chicken joints into a deep casserole with the soup and bay leaf. Cover the casserole and cook the chicken for about 2 hours, or until tender.

Just before serving take out of the oven, stir in the cream and sherry, taste and add more salt and pepper if necessary. Remove bay leaf, serve with freshly boiled rice, allowing 1½ to 2 oz. uncooked long-grain rice per person. Toss in a small packet of frozen peas with the rice for the last few minutes of the cooking time to add colour.

Coq au Vin* FOR THE GRAND OCCASION

FOR 6

3–4-lb. boiling fowl or, if not available, a roasting chicken of the same size; 1½ oz. butter; 1 tablespoon salad oil; 4 oz. smoked bacon trimmings, chopped; 12 whole small onions, peeled; 2 sticks celery, finely chopped; 6-oz. cup mushrooms, quartered; the chicken giblets, washed; 1 clove garlic, crushed; 1 oz. flour; ¾ pint cheap Burgundy; ¼ pint water; 1 bay leaf; 1 sprig fresh thyme or ¼ level teaspoon dried thyme; salt; pepper

To garnish: Small triangles of fried white bread

Preparation: 25 minutes *Cooking time: 1½–4 hours according to the age of the chicken*

Set oven at 325°F., Gas 3.

This is perhaps the most famous chicken dish in the world. In France each region seems to vary the recipe slightly, sometimes by adding a little brandy, sometimes by varying the herbs. An ideal dish for re-heating and therefore a good dish for entertaining.

Cut the chicken into 6 joints. Melt 1 oz. butter in a pan with the oil then fry the bacon trimmings until golden brown. Remove them from the pan and drain on kitchen paper. Fry the chicken joints on both sides – skin side first – until they are brown, then put them with the bacon trimmings. Fry the onion with the celery until they are soft then put them on one side. Melt the remaining fat in the pan and cook the mushrooms for about 2 minutes. Remove them from the pan and blend the crushed garlic and flour with the fat remaining in the pan. Cook it until the flour is brown, stirring frequently so that it does not burn. Remove the pan from the heat and blend in the wine a little at a time. Then add the water, bay leaf, thyme, salt and pepper, return the pan to the heat and simmer the liquid until it has thickened.

Pour it over the chicken joints, add the giblets to the casserole, cover with a lid and cook the chicken in the oven (325°F., Gas 3) for 1½–4 hours, depending on the size of the bird and whether it is a boiling or roasting chicken.

When the chicken joints are almost tender remove the giblets from the casserole, stir in the mushrooms and continue to cook for a further 10 minutes. Remove the casserole from the oven and skim off any excess fat with absorbent kitchen paper. Add more seasoning if required and serve garnished with the triangles of fried bread.

French Roast Chicken

FOR 4

2 oz. butter; 3-lb. roasting chicken; a few sprigs of parsley and a sprig of thyme; 2 rashers streaky bacon, de-rinded; ½ pint chicken stock or ½ pint water and a chicken stock cube

Preparation: 10 minutes *Cooking time: about 1 hour*

Set the oven at 400°F., Gas 6.

This is a good way of adding flavour to a young chicken.

Put 1 oz. of the butter inside the chicken with the herbs. Place the chicken in a roasting tin, rub with the remaining butter and cover the breast with the bacon. Pour the stock into the roasting tin.

Roast the chicken for 1 hour or until tender, basting frequently. Ten minutes before the end of cooking time remove the bacon so that the breast can brown. Remove the chicken from the tin, carve or cut into joints. Simmer the juices in the tin over a low heat until they are reduced to a syrupy consistency then strain them over the chicken.

Curried Chicken with Grapes* FOR THE GRAND OCCASION

FOR 4

2½–3-lb. roasting chicken; 1 small onion, peeled; 2 cloves; 2 small carrots; 1 bay leaf; sprig of parsley; 1 level teaspoon salt; 6 peppercorns; 1½ pints water

For the sauce: ¼ lb. white grapes; 1 oz. butter; 1 oz. flour; ½ pint stock from the chicken; 2 teaspoons red currant jelly; 1 level tablespoon curry powder; 5-oz. carton soured cream; salt; pepper

Preparation: 20 minutes *Cooking time: about 1 hour*

Chicken with a mild, curry-flavoured cream sauce.

Place the chicken in a large pan with the onion stuck with the cloves, the carrots, bay leaf, parsley, salt, peppercorns and water. Cover and simmer for 1 hour or until the chicken is tender. While the chicken is cooking skin and pip the grapes, put a few to one side for garnish.

Remove the chicken from the cooking liquor and leave to cool. Strain the stock and put it to one side. Skim off the surplus fat. Remove the flesh from the chicken and cut it into pieces, place in a serving dish and keep hot.

TO MAKE THE SAUCE: Melt the butter in a pan, stir in the curry powder and cook gently for 1 minute. Stir in the flour and cook for a further minute. Slowly blend in ½ pint of the stock. Stir until smooth, add red currant jelly, bring to boiling point and simmer for 2–3 minutes. Add the halved grapes, remove from the heat and add the cream. Adjust seasoning. Coat the chicken with the sauce, garnish with the remaining grapes. Goes well with boiled rice and a green salad.

Browned Chicken with Barbecue Sauce*

FOR 4

4 roasting chicken joints; ½ level teaspoon salt; ⅛ level teaspoon pepper; ½ level teaspoon caster sugar; ½ level teaspoon ground ginger; 1 oz. butter

Barbecue sauce: 1 tablespoon Worcestershire sauce; 2 level teaspoons caster sugar; 2 tablespoons distilled malt vinegar; 8 tablespoons tomato ketchup; 2 tablespoons soy sauce; 2 cloves garlic, crushed; 2 bay leaves; dash Tabasco sauce

Preparation: 20 minutes *Cooking time: about 40 minutes*

Set oven at 375°F., Gas 5.

This chicken goes well with buttered noodles or macaroni scattered with chopped parsley.

Put joints on a board. Mix together the salt, pepper, sugar and ginger and rub this mixture into the chicken. Heat the butter in a heavy meat tin and brown the joints in the oven for about 10 minutes, turning once to brown both sides.

While the joints are browning prepare the barbecue sauce: mix together all the ingredients in a bowl. When the joints are brown pour away all the fat from the tin then pour the sauce over the joints and cover the baking tin with a lid of foil. Bake for 20–30 minutes, basting occasionally, until the joints are tender. Arrange joints on a serving dish and remove bay leaves. Spoon the sauce over the chicken.

Fried Chicken with Creamed Corn

FOR 4

4 roasting chicken joints; 1 egg, beaten; dried, browned bread-crumbs; 4 tablespoons salad oil; 1 oz. butter

For the creamed corn: 11-oz. can corn kernels, drained; 2½-oz. carton single cream; salt and pepper

Preparation: 15 minutes *Cooking time: about 20 minutes*

A quick supper dish made in just the time it takes for the joints to fry. Potato crisps are easy and go well too.

Dip the chicken joints in the beaten egg and then coat them with breadcrumbs. Heat the oil in a frying pan then add the butter and allow it to melt. Brown the chicken joints on both sides over a fairly hot heat then reduce the heat, cover the pan with a lid and simmer the joints for 15 minutes or until they are tender.

Meanwhile prepare the creamed corn. Drain the corn kernels very well and put into a pan with the cream. Heat gently until piping hot then season to taste with salt and pepper. Put to one side to keep warm. As there is no acid present the cream will not curdle.

When the chicken joints are cooked remove them from the pan and arrange them on a serving dish with the creamed corn in the centre.

Chicken Simla*

FOR 4

1 oz. flour; salt; pepper; 4 roasting chicken joints; 2 tablespoons salad oil; 1 oz. butter; ½ pint single cream; ¼ pint chicken stock or ¼ pint water and ½ a chicken stock cube; 1 rounded tablespoon mild mustard; 2 teaspoons Worcestershire sauce; 1 oz. flaked, toasted almonds

Preparation: 15 minutes *Cooking time: about 1 hour*

Set oven at 325°F., Gas 3.

Literally chicken fried then simmered in a piquantly flavoured cream sauce.

Put the flour with the salt and pepper in a paper bag and put each joint in the bag one at a time. Shake until they are evenly coated with flour. Heat the oil in a pan, add the butter then fry the joints slowly until golden. Drain on kitchen paper and arrange in a greased shallow oven-proof dish.

In a bowl blend the cream, stock, mustard and Worcestershire sauce. Pour over the chicken. Scatter the almonds. Cover and bake for ¾ hour.

Goes well with purée potatoes and creamed spinach.

Chicken with Lemon Sauce

FOR 6

6 frying chicken joints; 1 oz. butter; 2 or 3 sprigs parsley; a sprig of lemon thyme or a pinch of dried thyme; thinly peeled rind and the juice of 2 lemons; water; 1 chicken stock cube

For the sauce: 1½ oz. butter; 1½ oz. flour; ½ pint milk; salt; pepper

Preparation: 20 minutes *Total cooking time: about 40 minutes*

Get out a meat tin.

Set the oven at 400°F., Gas 6.

Put the chicken joints into the meat tin, skin side upwards. Spread a little of the butter on each joint, then add the parsley, thyme, lemon rind and crumbled stock cube. Strain the lemon juice into a measuring jug and make it up to ½ pint with water. Pour this liquid over the joints and cook them uncovered in the pre-heated oven (400°F., Gas 6) for about 30 minutes, depending on size, basting occasionally, until they are tender and golden.

Remove the chicken joints from the meat tin and keep them hot while preparing the sauce. Strain off the liquor from the meat tin into a jug and skim off any excess fat. Melt the butter in a pan, blend in the flour and cook this roux over a low heat for 2 minutes, stirring frequently. Blend in the chicken liquor a little at a time away from the heat. Return the pan to the heat and bring the sauce to boiling point, stirring all the time. Simmer until the sauce has thickened then draw the pan away from the heat again and add the milk slowly. Return the pan to the heat and simmer the sauce for 2 or 3 minutes, stirring frequently, then season it with salt and pepper and pour it over the chicken joints.

SUPPER DISHES

These recipes are equally suitable for family lunches. Nasi Goreng and Paella, both rice classics, are ideal for a crowd.

Nasi Goreng

FOR 4

1 lb. boned shoulder of pork or lean pork chop trimmings; 3 oz. lard; ½ lb. onions, peeled and sliced; 8 oz. refined long-grain rice; about 3 pints water; 2 level teaspoons salt; 10-oz. packet frozen mixed vegetables; 2 tablespoons soy sauce; 1 level teaspoon curry powder; salt and pepper; 4 firm tomatoes; watercress or parsley. *For the pancake-like omelette to garnish:* 1 egg, beaten; 1 teaspoon water; salt; pepper; ¼ oz. butter

Preparation: 35 minutes *Cooking time: about 1¼ hours*

This is an Anglicized version of the well-known Indonesian dish. It is tremendous – and indeed my favourite rice dish. Nasi Goreng is a bit like a spicy risotto but moister. It's the sort of recipe that will make your girl friends rush out to the kitchen and scribble the recipe know-how on to the back of an envelope to try out for themselves.

Cut the pork into ½-in. thick slices then cut each slice into ½-in. cubes. Melt the lard in a fairly large pan (about 6 pints), add the pork and onions and fry quickly for 5 minutes. Reduce the heat, cover and cook for 30 minutes, stirring frequently so that the onions do not stick to the pan.

Meanwhile prepare the other ingredients. Put the water and salt into a pan, bring to boiling point, stir in the rice and simmer for 10–12 minutes or until the rice is barely cooked. Strain the rice into a sieve and rinse thoroughly with hot water to remove the excess starch. Leave to drain. Cook the frozen vegetables according to the directions on the packet and drain well.

Make the omelette: mix together the egg and water and season with salt and pepper. Melt the butter in a small frying pan, pour in the egg mixture and make a thin, flat, pancake-like omelette. When the underside is brown turn the omelette over and cook for a further minute. Remove from the pan and shred into ¼-in. strips.

When the pork is tender stir in the soy sauce and curry powder and the rice, mixing well. Lastly stir in the vegetables. Add plenty of salt and pepper to season. Arrange on a serving dish with the shredded omelette strips piled on top and the tomatoes, cut in wedges, round the edge, flash under the grill. Garnish with watercress or parsley. Serve with a green salad.

IF PREPARING BEFOREHAND: In the morning cook the pork and onions, add soy sauce, curry powder. Make the flat omelette and cut tomatoes.

20 MINUTES BEFORE THE MEAL: Boil the rice and mixed vegetables. Heat pork and onions, mix with rice then vegetables. Season, garnish with omelette strips and tomato wedges and flash under the grill.

Sherried Kidneys*

FOR THE GRAND OCCASION

FOR 4

8 lambs' kidneys or 5 pigs' kidneys; 2 oz. butter; 1 medium onion, peeled and finely chopped; 1 oz. flour; ½ pint stock or ½ pint water and ½ beef stock cube; 6 tablespoons dry sherry; 1 heaped teaspoon French mustard; little Worcestershire sauce; salt; pepper; little gravy browning; 1 tablespoon chopped parsley

Preparation: 15 minutes *Cooking time: 15 minutes*

Goes well with boiled rice or almost any pasta.

Remove the fat and skin from the kidneys then cut them in half lengthwise and remove the cores. If using pigs' kidneys cut each in about 8 slices. Melt 1 oz. of the butter in a pan and fry the onion slowly until it is pale brown and soft. Add the kidneys and continue to cook for about 2 minutes on each side until the kidneys have become firm and are just turning brown. Remove the onion and kidneys from the pan and keep them hot. Melt the remaining butter in the pan, blend in the flour, then add the stock, blending it until it is smooth. Stir in the sherry, mustard, Worcestershire sauce, salt and pepper then bring the sauce to boiling point, stirring all the time until it has thickened. Return the onion and kidneys to the pan, cover and simmer for 5 minutes or until the kidneys are just cooked. Check the seasoning, add a little gravy browning for a good colour, pour the kidneys and sauce into a serving dish and sprinkle with chopped parsley.

Spanish Omelette*

FOR 2

2 large, whole firm cooked potatoes (about 8 oz.); 1 large Spanish onion, peeled; 1 small green pepper; 2 tablespoons salad oil; 4 eggs; 4 teaspoons cold water; salt; pepper; ½ oz. butter; chopped parsley

Preparation: 15 minutes *Cooking time: about 15 minutes*

Cut the potatoes into ½-in. squares and chop the onion coarsely. Cut the pepper in half, remove the seeds and stalk then cut it into ¼-in. wide slices. Put the frying-pan, which should be about 7–8 in. across the base, on a low heat, pour in the oil and heat, then prepare the omelette egg mixture. Break the eggs into a bowl, add the water and seasoning and beat lightly with a fork until well blended. Fry the onion slowly in the oil until it is soft, turn the heat up, add the pepper and potato. Allow the vegetables to brown lightly, sprinkle with salt and pepper. Then add the butter and pour in the egg mixture. Stir, drawing the mixture from the sides to the middle of the pan to allow the uncooked egg to set quickly. When the underside is firm and the top still runny, flash it under a hot grill for a moment until the omelette is just set. Cut into two and slide each half on to a hot plate. Sprinkle with chopped parsley and serve with a green salad.

Quiche Lorraine

FOR 6

Shortcrust pastry: 6 oz. plain flour; 2 oz. butter; 1½ oz. lard; pinch salt; about 6 teaspoons water.
Filling: 4 oz. Gruyère cheese, finely sliced; 4 rashers streaky bacon, de-rinded; ¼ pint single cream; 2 large eggs; 1 teaspoon chopped parsley; 1 teaspoon chopped chives or green onion tops; salt; pepper

Preparation: 25 minutes *Total cooking time: about 45 minutes*

Get out a shallow, 9-in. fluted flan case or ring.
Set oven at 425°F., Gas 7.

FOR THE PASTRY: Sift the flour and salt into a bowl. Cut the fats into small pieces then rub into the flour until the mixture resembles fine breadcrumbs. Add enough water to mix to a firm dough. Roll out thinly on a well-floured board. Line the flan case with the pastry, chill for half an hour or so in the refrigerator before baking, if time allows. Place a piece of greaseproof paper on top of the pastry case and fill with baking beans (or, alternatively, use a large piece of kitchen foil, crumpled). Bake for about 15 minutes at 425°F., Gas 7 until the pastry edge is pale golden then remove the paper and beans or foil.

Re-set oven at 350°F., Gas 4.

Arrange the cheese slices in the bottom of the flan case, fry or grill the bacon very lightly for 1–2 minutes, cut each rasher in half and arrange in spoke fashion on top of the cheese. Mix together the cream, eggs, parsley and chives. Add salt and pepper to taste. Pour the mixture into the flan case and bake for 30 minutes or until pale golden and just set. Serve hot or cold.

Smoked Haddock Kedgeree

FOR 4

1 lb. smoked haddock; 1 pint water; 1½ oz. butter; 6 oz. refined long-grain rice; salt; pepper; 1 tablespoon chopped parsley; pinch grated nutmeg; 2 hard-boiled eggs, sliced; 1 egg, beaten (optional)

Preparation: 15 minutes *Total cooking time: about 25 minutes*

Set the oven at 325°F., Gas 3.

This dish can be made in advance and reheated with no effort but if it is prepared to coincide with punctual guests it is a great improvement to bind a raw egg and a little top of the milk into the cooked rice and fish, so long as the dish is not left too long in the oven.

Put the haddock and water into a pan and bring to simmering point. Simmer it for about 10 minutes (it should not boil) or until the haddock is barely cooked. Take it out of the water and remove the skin and bones. Put the flaked fish into an oven-proof serving dish with 1 oz. of the butter, cover it and keep it warm at 325°F., Gas 3. Add the rice to the water in which the fish has been cooked, bring to boiling point and boil for about 10–12 minutes or until the rice is just cooked. Drain it and add it to the fish. Add plenty of salt and pepper, parsley, nutmeg, most of the hard-boiled egg and the beaten egg and top of the milk if used. Decorate the kedgeree with the remaining hard-boiled egg and a little more parsley.

Shrimp and Fish Pie*

FOR 6

1 oz. butter; 1½ lb. cod fillets; salt; pepper
For the sauce: 1½ oz. butter; 1½ oz. flour; about ½ pint milk; 2 teaspoons anchovy essence; 4 oz. frozen shrimps or prawns
For the topping: 1½ lb. potatoes, cooked and mashed in the usual way

Preparation: 20 minutes *Total cooking time: about 1 hour*

Get out a 2½–3-pint oven-proof serving dish.

Set oven at 325°F., Gas 3.

Spread the dish with half the butter, then put the cod in the dish and sprinkle it with salt and pepper. Put the rest of the butter, cut in very small pieces, on top of the fish. Cover with a lid or foil and cook for 20 to 30 minutes, or until the fish will flake easily. Remove the dish from the oven and strain the liquor from it into a measuring jug.

Remove the skin and any bones from the fish and put the flesh into a bowl. Melt the butter for the sauce in a pan, blend in the flour and cook this roux for 1 minute. Add enough milk to the fish liquor to make it up to ¾ pint, then blend it slowly with the roux to make a smooth sauce. Bring it to boiling point and let it simmer for 2 minutes, stirring constantly. Blend in the anchovy essence, prawns, and enough salt and pepper to season the sauce well. Stir the sauce into the flaked fish and then turn it into the clean oven-proof dish.

Spread the prepared, mashed potato over the fish. Mark it with a fork to make a neat pattern. Increase the oven temperature to

400°F., Gas 6. Reheat the pie for about 20 minutes until it is piping hot and the top is golden brown.

If time is short, blend a condensed celery soup with the fish juices instead of preparing a sauce.

Paella

FOR THE GRAND OCCASION

FOR 8

4 tablespoons salad oil; ¾ lb. chicken meat, cubed, or 8 drum sticks; 4 oz. bacon or pork cut in ½-in. squares; 2 medium onions, peeled and roughly chopped; 1 clove garlic; sprig fresh thyme; 1 quart fresh mussels in their shells; ⅛ pint white wine; 10 oz. refined, long-grain rice; pinch saffron powder; 4–6 oz. halibut or firm fish, skinned, boned and cut into ¾-in. pieces; 4 oz. sliced garlic sausage; 1¼ pints liquid – mussel liquor with chicken stock or water; 3 level teaspoons salt; ¼ level teaspoon freshly milled pepper; 4 oz. shelled prawns; 3 tomatoes, skinned and pipped; 8 oz. cooked peas; 8 whole large cooked Mediterranean prawns; 1 small can sweet red peppers, drained and sliced; 1 sliced, blanched green pepper; 8 stuffed green olives; 2 teaspoons coarsely chopped parsley; lemon wedges.

Preparation: 35 minutes *Cooking time: about 45 minutes*

As we know roast beef and Yorkshire pudding, the Spaniards know paella. Each region has its own variation – near the sea you'll find they use more seafood – don't worry if you can't get all the ingredients, add more or less fish and meat to balance.

Measure oil into paellera or large oven-proof open pan. Fry chicken meat, bacon or pork and onions until pale golden brown. Then add crushed garlic and thyme.

Rinse mussels, using only tightly closed ones, clean and scrub well, put in a pan with a tightly fitting lid with white wine, season and simmer until they steam open; not more than five minutes. Scoop out the mussels from their shells using an empty shell to push each out. Keep 8 shells for decoration. Add to the paellera the rice, saffron, halibut, halved slices of garlic sausage and liquid. Blend well together with spoon, add pepper and salt, bring to the boil on top of the stove. Cover with foil and bake, stirring from time to time, for about 25 minutes at 350°F., Gas 4, until the rice is barely soft. Remove from the oven and stir in shelled prawns, tomatoes, peas, de-shelled mussels and some of the pepper slices. Arrange on the top the large Mediterranean prawns, mussels and remainder of the peppers, cover with foil and return to the oven for a further 10 minutes.

Before serving, add the olives and sprinkle the whole dish with parsley. Serve the paella with wedges of lemon.

Moussaka*

FOR 6

4 large aubergines; ¼ level teaspoon salt; 1½ lb. onions; 1 clove garlic; 16-oz. can tomatoes; salad oil; 1½ lb. coarsely minced shoulder lamb; 1 oz. flour; 1½ level teaspoons salt; ⅛ teaspoon pepper; ¼ teaspoon mixed dried herbs; 2 tablespoons chopped parsley

Cheese Sauce: 1 oz. butter; 1½ oz. flour; ¾ pint milk; 1 level teaspoon made mustard; 6 oz. strong Cheddar cheese, grated; pepper; salt

Preparation: 30 minutes *Total cooking time: about 1¼ hours*

Set oven at 375°F., Gas 5.

Moussaka is an untemperamental supper or buffet dish. It can be reheated most satisfactorily and is the best way I know of using up a cold lamb joint. In this recipe I have used freshly minced lamb but it could equally well be cooked minced lamb.

Slice unpeeled aubergines in ½-in. rounds. Sprinkle with salt, leave for half an hour, then drain off liquid. Chop onions roughly and chop garlic very finely. Strain tomatoes and save juice.

Fry aubergines in oil, using as little as possible, lift on to kitchen paper. Take a large heavy saucepan and heat a tablespoon of oil, add meat, stir and allow to brown, then add onions and garlic and cook over heat for 10 minutes.

Whilst this is cooking make cheese sauce. Melt butter in pan, add flour, cook together over medium heat without browning for about 2 minutes. Draw pan to one side, blend in milk, mixing slowly, return to the heat, bring to the boil and add cheese, mustard, pepper, salt. Allow cheese to dissolve.

Blend in flour with meat mixture, add salt, pepper, tomato juice, herbs and parsley, saving a little for sprinkling before serving. Butter a shallow oven-proof dish. Arrange layers of aubergines, meat mixture and tomato, finish with a circular pattern of aubergine slices. Pour cheese sauce over.

Bake and allow to brown in the oven (375°F., Gas 5) for about 45 minutes. Scatter with parsley and serve with hot French bread and butter.

Molly's Spaghetti

FOR 4

8 oz. spaghetti; ¼ lb. streaky bacon or whatever you have in the fridge, de-rinded; ½ oz. butter; 6 oz. button mushrooms, sliced; 1 good tablespoon chopped parsley; 2 eggs, beaten; salt and pepper; grated Parmesan cheese

Preparation: 10 minutes *Cooking time: 15 minutes*

Cook the spaghetti in plenty of boiling salted water for 12 minutes or until it is just tender then drain it well and return it to the pan.

Whilst the spaghetti is cooking cut the bacon rashers into ½-in. wide strips. Melt the butter in a pan and fry the bacon until it is pale golden brown. Add the mushrooms and cook them for 2 minutes then blend the bacon and mushroom mixture into the cooked spaghetti. Stir in the parsley (saving a little for topping), eggs, pepper and salt. Cook over a low heat, stirring with a fork, until the eggs have scrambled. Pile on to a serving dish and sprinkle the top of the spaghetti with Parmesan cheese and chopped parsley.

Lasagne Al Forno*

FOR 8

This Italian dish is made of layers of spicy Ragu Bolognese sauce, lasagne – wide pasta ribbons – and a creamy white Bechamel sauce. The top is crisp and brown, and generously scattered with grated cheese. In Italy Mozzarella cheese is used, but this cheese is not always available as it is a cheese that must be eaten fresh; excellent substitutes are Gruyère or Bel Paese. Make the Ragu Bolognese sauce and leave it to simmer for one hour. Then make the Bechamel sauce and keep it hot. Finally boil the lasagne, assemble dish, top with cheese. To cook this quantity you will need one large 4-pint shallow oven-proof dish, well buttered.

Preparation: 40 minutes *Total cooking time: 2 hours*

STAGE ONE

RAGU BOLOGNESE SAUCE

4 oz. streaky bacon, chopped; 1 lb. lean beef, minced; 3 medium onions, chopped; 4 tablespoons oil; 4 sticks celery, chopped (or 1 teaspoon dried celery flakes); 2 cloves garlic, pressed or finely chopped; 2 pinches mixed herbs; 4 level teaspoons salt; 1 teaspoon sugar; $\frac{1}{4}$ teaspoon ground black pepper; 5-oz. can tomato purée; $\frac{3}{4}$ pint water

In a large frying-pan slowly fry the bacon, beef and onion in the oil until brown, stirring frequently. Add the celery, garlic, herbs, salt, sugar, pepper, tomato purée and water. Cover and simmer for 1 hour.

STAGE TWO

BECHAMEL SAUCE

1 pint milk; 1 bay leaf; 3 peppercorns; 2 blades mace; parsley stalks; 1 small carrot; piece onion; $1\frac{1}{2}$ oz. butter; $1\frac{1}{2}$ oz. flour; salt; pepper

Slowly heat the milk in the pan with the bay leaf, peppercorns, mace, parsley stalks, carrot and onion. Cover, simmer gently for 10 minutes then strain. Melt the butter in a saucepan, add the flour and seasoning. Stir over a low heat for a few minutes, then draw to one side and slowly incorporate the milk, stirring briskly. Return sauce to the heat, bring it to the boil, and allow it to thicken. Adjust the seasoning, lower the heat, cover the sauce and keep it hot.

STAGE THREE

TO COOK THE LASAGNE

1 tablespoon oil; 1 level tablespoon salt; 12 oz. lasagne; 6 oz. Gruyère cheese, grated, for sprinkling over each layer of Bechamel sauce; 2 oz. Parmesan cheese, grated, for the topping

In a large saucepan bring 8 pints water, the oil and tablespoon of salt to the boil. Carefully and quickly put the lasagne into the water, a piece at a time, and boil it for 8 minutes or until barely tender. Drain it in a colander, refresh it with cold water, then arrange it on a clean, damp tea towel so that the pieces do not stick together.

Assemble the dish in three layers, starting with a layer of Ragu Bolognese sauce, then a layer of pasta, then a layer of Bechamel sauce and grated Gruyère cheese. Continue in this way, ending with a layer of Bechamel sauce. Sprinkle with the remaining Gruyère and the Parmesan. Bake at 350°F., Gas 4, for 40 minutes, until the top is pale golden.

Cheese Soufflé, Hot

A hot soufflé is only a glorified white sauce, and you should find it perfectly easy to manage. But there are three important points to remember.

First, you must have the right amount of mixture for the dish. For the recipe below you will need a 2-pint soufflé dish to get a well-risen soufflé; if you use a dish of the wrong size, your soufflé will not be so successful.

Secondly, you must fold the not too stiffly whisked egg whites into the soufflé mixture at the last moment before baking.

Lastly, you must have your guests sitting at table before you take it out of the oven.

The quantities I have given are enough for four people as a first course, or for two or three hungry people as a main course.

FOR 3

$1\frac{1}{2}$ oz. butter; $1\frac{1}{2}$ oz. flour; $\frac{1}{2}$ pint milk; $\frac{1}{2}$ teaspoon prepared mustard; $\frac{1}{4}$ level teaspoon grated nutmeg; 2 oz. dry Cheddar cheese and 2 oz. Parmesan cheese (or 4 oz. dry Cheddar cheese), grated; 3 large eggs, separated; salt and pepper

Preparation: 15 minutes *Cooking time: about 40 minutes*

You will need a 2-pint soufflé dish. Set oven at 350°F., Gas 4.

Butter the soufflé dish and set it on one side. Melt the butter in a pan, then remove the pan from the heat and blend in the flour. Return the pan to the heat and cook the roux (butter and flour mixture) for 1 minute, stirring all the time so that it does not turn brown. Remove the pan from the heat again and add the milk a little at a time, stirring well so that no lumps form. Bring the sauce to boiling point and then let it simmer until it is thick and smooth, stirring constantly. Remove the pan from the heat and beat in the mustard, nutmeg and cheese; when these are well incorporated in the sauce stir in the egg yolks one by one. Add salt and pepper.

Whisk the egg whites with a wire or rotary whisk until peaks will just form and tip over when they are lifted up on the whisk. The white should look smooth and shiny, not dry and stiff. Using a metal spoon, fold a heaped tablespoon of the egg white into the white sauce mixture, then fold in the remaining egg white using a figure of eight movement and working the soufflé mixture as little as possible so that air is not knocked out of it.

Pour the soufflé into the buttered dish. There is no need to tie a collar of greaseproof paper round the dish, because your soufflé will rise up straight if the next step is carefully followed.

Run the tip of a teaspoon round the outside edge of the soufflé, scooping the soufflé mixture towards the centre (this will make it rise in the middle), then bake it in the pre-heated oven (350°F., Gas 4) for 40 minutes. Serve immediately—a soufflé waits for no one!

FOR THE COLD TABLE

When there's a gathering of the clans there's a need for main meal dishes that can be produced all ready prepared a day or so in advance. Boiled bacon is versatile because not only can you have it cold but you can buy a really large piece, bake it and have it hot first, then slice it cold the next day with salads, and when all the revelling is over the family can have bacon omelettes or what have you.

Mustard Baked Gammon in Cider* FOR THE GRAND OCCASION

FOR 8

5-lb. piece boned and rolled gammon; 2 bay leaves; 6 peppercorns; 1 piece root ginger; 1 carrot; 1 large onion, peeled; 1 pint dry cider; water

For topping: 2 oz. soft brown sugar; 1 level tablespoon dry mustard

Preparation: 15 minutes *Cooking time: about 2 hours simmering and 15 minutes browning*

Soak the joint overnight in plenty of cold water to remove the excess salt. Place the joint in a large pan on top of the stove with the bay leaves, peppercorns, ginger, carrot and onion. Pour in cider, add water till the joint is covered and bring to the boil. Put a lid on the pan and simmer the joint gently for 20 minutes to the pound plus an extra 20 minutes. Cool the gammon in the cooking liquid overnight. Peel off the skin and, with a sharp knife, score the fat in lines at $\frac{1}{4}$-in. intervals. Mix together the sugar and mustard and sprinkle it over, and press into, the fat surface of the joint. Put the joint into a meat tin, lightly brush with a little oil or butter, brown the joint in the oven (400°F., Gas 6), until golden.

Chicken Indienne à la Crème* FOR THE GRAND OCCASION

FOR 6

Chicken: Rind of 1 lemon; 3–4-lb. chicken; 1 onion; 1 blade of mace; 6 peppercorns; sprig thyme; parsley stalks; 1½ level teaspoons salt; about 1½ pints water
Sauce: 2 oz. butter; 1½ oz. plain flour; 1 level tablespoon curry powder; 1 pint chicken stock; 2 level tablespoons red currant jelly; ¼ pint double cream; salt and pepper for seasoning
Garnish: Paprika pepper; few endive leaves; parsley and poppadums

Preparation: 20 minutes *Cooking time: about 1½ hours*

Peel lemon thinly using a potato peeler. In a saucepan place chicken, onion, mace, peppercorns, thyme, parsley stalks, lemon rind, salt and water. Cover and bring to the boil, simmer until tender, approximately 1–1½ hours. Allow chicken to cool in stock. Take chicken from pan, remove meat from bones and cut into pieces. Skim fat off stock and strain.

TO MAKE SAUCE: melt butter, add flour and curry powder, cook for a few minutes. Draw to one side of the heat and slowly add 1 pint stock from chicken, beating well. Return to the heat, bring to the boil and allow to thicken, stirring all the time. Blend in red currant jelly. Cool. While cooling whisk from time to time. Add cream and then the chopped chicken and adjust seasoning.

Leave 6 hours before serving for flavours to blend.

Shake over paprika pepper and decorate with endive and parsley. Serve with fried poppadums and salad.

Raised Chicken and Ham Pie*

FOR 8

For the filling: 2½–3-lb. chicken; ½ pint bacon stock (or 1 ham bone, or failing this, smoked bacon rinds to add flavour to the chicken stock); 1 onion, peeled; 1 bay leaf; 6 peppercorns; 4 blades mace; 2 sprigs of thyme; about 2–3 pints water; ¾ lb. cooked, lean boiled bacon; 2 hard-boiled eggs; 1 oz. powdered gelatine; salt; pepper

For the shortcrust pastry: 14 oz. plain flour; 1 level teaspoon salt; 3½ oz. butter; 3½ oz. lard; about 4 tablespoons cold water
For the egg glaze: 1 egg, beaten; 1 tablespoon cold water

Preparation: 35 minutes *Total cooking time: about 2 hours 40 minutes*

Get out a 2½-pint capacity loaf tin.
Set oven at 425°F., Gas 7.

Put the chicken into a pan with the bacon stock, or ham bone or bacon rinds. Also add the onion, bay leaf, peppercorns, mace and thyme. Cover with water, put the lid on the pan and simmer the chicken for 1 to 2½ hours, or until tender, depending on the age of the bird. Remove the chicken from the pan and put it to one side to cool. Strain the cooking liquor into another pan and reduce it to 1 pint by boiling it hard. Remove the flesh from the chicken and cut it into small pieces. Cut the bacon into ½-in. cubes.

Prepare the short crust pastry. Sift the flour and salt into a bowl, cut the fats into small pieces and rub them into the flour until the mixture resembles fine breadcrumbs. Add enough water to mix to a firm dough. Roll out the pastry about ⅛-in. thick on a lightly floured board. Using the loaf tin as a guide cut out two oblong pieces of pastry for the top and bottom of the pie. Put these on one side. Re-roll the pastry if necessary and cut out two strips, each the same depth as the tin and each long enough to go half-way round the loaf tin. Use the pastry trimmings to make six pastry leaves and a rose. Cut a strip of pastry 1¾ in. wide for the leaves, then cut the strip into six diamond shapes and mark each diamond with the back of a knife to form 'veins'. Cut another strip of pastry 4 by 1½ in. Make ½-in. deep cuts along one long edge of the strip, then roll it up and pull the cut edges back to form a flower. Place one of the oblong pieces of pastry in the base. Brush the edges with egg glaze. Press the pastry strips round the sides of the tin, making sure that the bottom edges of the pastry strips are slightly overlapping to join to the moistened edge of the base of the pie.

FOR THE FILLING: In a bowl mix together the chicken and bacon, add 2 level teaspoons salt and ¼ level teaspoon freshly ground black pepper. Put half the meat into the pie tin. Place the shelled eggs on top of the meat, then put the remaining meat on top of the eggs and press it down firmly. Brush the top edge of the pie with egg glaze and place the remaining piece of pastry on top. Press the edges together to seal them firmly. Make a small hole in the centre of the pie. Brush the top of the pie with egg glaze, then brush the pastry leaves with egg glaze and place them on top, curving them slightly. Put the pastry 'rose' into the hole in the pie and brush it carefully with glaze. Bake the pie in the pre-heated oven (425°F., Gas 7) for about 50 minutes until golden brown, brushing the top once with more glaze. If the top of the pie becomes too brown at this stage, cover it with a piece of foil.

While the pie is cooking put the gelatine into a bowl with 8 tablespoons cooled stock taken from the 1 pint cooking liquor. Place the bowl over a pan of hot water and leave the gelatine to dissolve. Then stir the dissolved gelatine into the remaining stock, taste it and add more salt and pepper as required so that it is really well seasoned. Leave it in a cold place until it is cold but not set.

When the pie is cooked remove it from the oven and very carefully remove the rose from the centre of the pie, using a small sharp knife. Allow the pie to cool for 15 minutes, remove from the tin then insert a small funnel into the centre of the pie and slowly pour in the cold stock. When the pie will contain no more stock replace the rose in the centre, put the pie into the refrigerator overnight to become firm. Next day serve with a fresh English salad.

Orange Stuffed Duck Galantine*

FOR THE GRAND OCCASION

FOR 6

One duck about 4½–5 lb.; ½ teaspoon salt; ¼ level teaspoon freshly ground black pepper; ¼ level teaspoon dried rosemary; ½ level teaspoon dried marjoram; 3 oranges; 1½ oz. butter; the duck liver; 6 oz. pork trimmings; 6 oz. pie veal; 2 oz. streaky bacon, de-rinded; 2 tablespoons brandy; ½ pint white wine

Preparation: 35 minutes *Cooking time: about 2¼ hours*

Get out a meat tin; string; a larding needle or large darning needle.

Set oven at 325°F., Gas 3.

To bone a duck takes time but is not difficult. Put the duck, breast side down, on a wooden board. With a sharp knife cut through the back skin and cut through to the backbone, then carefully work the flesh away from the carcass, pressing the knife closely against the carcass and taking all the meat away from the bone with the skin. Be careful not to split the skin. Remove the bones from the legs and wings by scraping the flesh away from the bones, keeping the skin whole if possible. Leave the drumstick bone in place. Remove any excess fat from the boned duck then sprinkle it with half the salt and pepper and all of the herbs. Peel the oranges so that all the white pith is removed, then cut each orange in half. Melt the butter in a small pan and fry the duck liver for 2 minutes on each side, then remove it from the pan. Mince the liver, pork, veal and bacon coarsely, put them in a bowl and mix them with the remaining salt and pepper, the brandy and 1 tablespoon of the wine. Spread half of the stuffing on the duck then lay the orange halves along the centre of the duck with their cut sides uppermost. Spread the remaining stuffing on top of the oranges. Fold in the ends of the duck then fold the sides into the centre to form a 'parcel'. Sew together with fine string to keep the duck in shape. Turn the duck breast side up and place it in the meat tin with the rest of the wine. Roast it in the pre-heated oven (325°F., Gas 3) basting it occasionally, for 2¼ hours or until the duck is deep golden brown. Remove it from the oven and allow it to become cold in the tin overnight. To serve, remove the duck from the meat tin and cut it into thin slices.

Crab and Salmon Mousse*

FOR 6

7¾-oz. can pink salmon; 6½-oz. can crab; about ½ pint milk; 1 oz. butter; 1 oz. flour; 1 tablespoon anchovy essence; ½ cucumber, peeled and finely diced; ½ oz. powdered gelatine; 3 tablespoons cold water; ¼ pint double cream; ¼ pint single cream

Preparation: 15 minutes

Get out 6 individual serving dishes or a 2-pint serving dish.

Drain the liquid from the cans of salmon and crab into a measuring jug. Make up to ½ pint with milk.

Melt the butter in a saucepan, blend in the flour and cook this roux for 1 minute. Remove the pan from the heat and stir in milk.

Bring to boiling point, stirring constantly. Simmer the sauce for 2 minutes, then remove from the heat and allow to cool slightly, stirring frequently so that a skin does not form on the top.

Remove the skin and bones from the salmon. Add the crab, mash them with a fork, then stir them into the sauce with the anchovy essence and diced cucumber. Put the gelatine with the water into a bowl placed over a pan of simmering water. When it has dissolved, remove it from the heat and blend it in to the sauce. Leave the sauce in a cool place, stirring it occasionally, until it is on the point of setting. Whip the two creams together until they form soft peaks, then fold the cream into the mixture. Taste it and add enough salt and pepper to season it well.

Turn the mousse into the individual dishes or one large dish and leave it in a cold place to set.

Salmon in Aspic* FOR THE GRAND OCCASION

FOR 8

3½-lb. piece of tail salmon; 2 pints water; 6 tablespoons tarragon or wine vinegar; 1 small onion, peeled and chopped; 6 peppercorns; a blade of mace; 2 level teaspoons salt; 1 bay leaf; parsley; thinly-peeled rind of 1 lemon

Home-made lemon aspic: ½ pint water; 1 oz. powdered gelatine; 2 tablespoons lemon juice; 2 tablespoons tarragon vinegar; 2 level tablespoons caster sugar; 1 level teaspoon salt

For garnish: ½ cucumber

Preparation: 30 minutes *Cooking time: 1 hour*

Get out a large meat tin and a piece of foil 24 by 48 in.

Set the oven at 325°F., Gas 3.

Get the fishmonger to clean the fish, or do it yourself by cleaning it through the gills, scraping inside the salmon, especially near the backbone. Butter the foil and use it to line the meat tin, with the buttered side uppermost. Lift the salmon into the lined tin.

Put the water and all the seasonings in a pan, bring it to boiling point then remove it from the heat and allow the contents to cool slightly before pouring them over the fish inside the foil. You may find that there is some liquid over, as this will depend on the size of the tin. Fold the foil over the fish without it actually touching the fish, or the skin will stick to the foil. Cook the salmon in the preheated oven for about an hour. The oven must not be too hot or the skin of the salmon will crack. When the salmon is done the flesh will be opaque and when pricked with a skewer the liquid that pours out should be almost colourless.

Remove the salmon from the oven, baste it with the liquid and leave it in the tin to cool completely.

Lift the cold salmon on to a wooden board and, with a sharp pointed knife, make a V-shaped cut above the tail. Then strip off the skin carefully, leaving the skin on the tail.

Prepare the aspic and while it is being made put the fish into a cold place to chill, as this makes the aspic set instantly when spooned over the fish. To make the aspic put ½ pint water into a small pan with the gelatine and leave it to soak for 5 minutes. Then heat it slowly, without simmering at all, until the gelatine has dissolved and the liquid is clear. Remove the pan from the heat, add the lemon juice, vinegar, sugar and salt. Stir, then allow the aspic to cool until it is just beginning to thicken.

Put the chilled salmon on to a wire rack with a tray underneath to catch the drips and spoon about half of the aspic over the fish so that all of it is evenly coated with glaze.

Arrange a decoration. This can be just thinly sliced cucumber arranged all along the back or more elaborate if you wish, then cover the decoration with aspic.

If the aspic has become too set place it over a low heat and allow it to dissolve. Then spoon it over the decorated fish, including the tail. The aspic should be more runny for this coat than for the first coat of aspic. Leave the fish in a cold place to set before serving.

Serve cold with cucumber salad and mayonnaise.

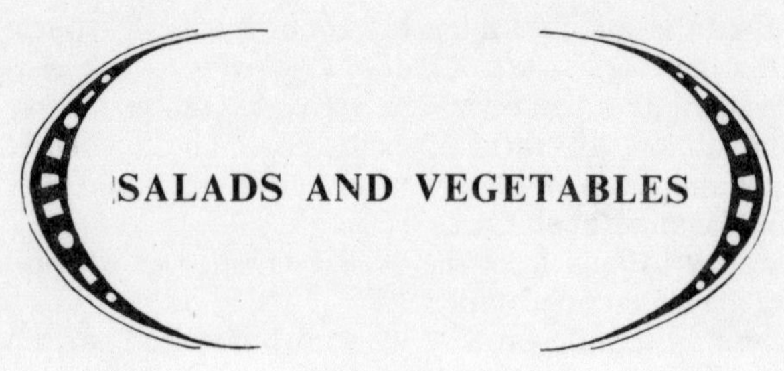

SALADS AND VEGETABLES

These are some unusual salad ideas and different ways of serving vegetables. The first five vegetable recipes are excellent for the cook-cum-hostess as they cook themselves in the oven and need no last-minute attention.

Potato, Apple and Celery Salad*

FOR 6

1 lb. boiled potatoes; 6 tablespoons French dressing (page 64); 1 small head celery, chopped; 1 large dessert apple, quartered, cored and diced; ¼ pint mayonnaise, preferably home-made; salt; pepper; 1 tablespoon chopped chives

Preparation: 15 minutes

Slice the hot potatoes into a bowl. Blend in the French dressing and leave on one side until the potatoes are cold. Then add the celery and apple. Blend in the mayonnaise and plenty of seasoning. Add most of the chives, saving some to sprinkle over the top. Cover the bowl and leave it in a cold place until the salad is required. Just before serving sprinkle with the remaining chives.

Note: This salad is excellent when made with a can of new potatoes. Drain them thoroughly before use and omit the dressing from the recipe.

Sweetcorn and Soured Cream Salad*

FOR 4

11-oz. can sweetcorn kernels, well drained; 2 or 3 spring onions, finely chopped; 5-oz. carton soured cream; salt; pepper
For the decoration: green and red peppers, sliced

Preparation: 10 minutes

Put the well-drained sweetcorn in a bowl with the onions. Blend in the soured cream and season well with plenty of salt and pepper. Turn the salad into a serving dish. Decorate round the edge with slices of green and red peppers.

Note: If you have some cooked peas left over from a previous meal these may also be added.

Spiced Coleslaw*

FOR 4–6

1 lb. firm white cabbage; 2 oz. caster sugar; 1 oz. plain flour; ½ oz. or 1 level tablespoon dry mustard; 1 level teaspoon salt; 1 oz. butter; 2 egg yolks; ⅛ pint vinegar; ⅛ pint single cream; 1 large carrot, grated; ½ oz. sultanas; 1 oz. seedless raisins; pepper

Preparation: 15 minutes *Cooking time: about 10 minutes*

Shred the cabbage finely, discarding the thick stems. Mix together the sugar, flour, mustard and salt in a bowl. Stand the bowl over a pan of simmering water, add the butter, egg yolks and vinegar. Stir constantly. When the mixture has thickened remove the bowl from the heat. When it is cold blend in the cream. Stir in to the cabbage. Add the carrots, sultanas and raisins. Season with plenty of pepper and more salt if necessary.

Beetroot and Horseradish Salad

FOR 4

1 to 1¼ lb. cooked beetroot, peeled; 3 tablespoons horseradish cream; 1 dessert apple, peeled, cored and diced
For the dressing: ½ level teaspoon salt; ⅛ level teaspoon pepper;

½ level teaspoon caster sugar; 1 tablespoon salad oil; ½ tablespoon white wine vinegar

Preparation: 10 minutes

Cut the beetroot in small cubes. Put it into a bowl. Blend in the horseradish cream and apple.

Blend together all the ingredients for the dressing. Mix with the other ingredients. Add more salt and pepper if necessary. Leave the salad, covered, in a cold place until needed.

Tomato and Onion Salad*

FOR 4

1 lb. firm tomatoes; 2 medium-sized onions, peeled; 4 tablespoons French dressing; 1 tablespoon chopped parsley

Preparation: 10 minutes

Get out a shallow serving dish.

Plunge the tomatoes in a pan of boiling water for 10 seconds, then drain them and rinse with cold water. Remove the skins and cut the tomatoes in slices. Slice the onions very finely. Arrange the tomato and onion slices in neat layers in the dish, finishing with a layer of tomato. Spoon over the French dressing, cover and leave in a cold place until required. Just before serving sprinkle with the chopped parsley.

Piquant Chicken and Rice Salad* FOR THE GRAND OCCASION

FOR 4–6

3-lb. roasting chicken; 8 oz. long-grain rice; 8-oz. can pineapple cubes; salt; 1 oz. sultanas; 1 oz. seedless raisins; 1 small onion, finely chopped; 4 oz. button mushrooms; 10-oz. packet frozen peas, cooked

For the dressing: 2 level teaspoons caster sugar; 3 level teaspoons salt; 1 teaspoon made mustard; ¼ level teaspoon freshly ground black pepper; 6 tablespoons salad oil; 2 tablespoons white wine vinegar

For decoration: ½ oz. butter; 1 oz. flaked almonds

Preparation: 20 minutes *Cooking time: about 1 hour*

Roast the chicken in the usual way, or buy a pre-cooked chicken. Put it on one side to cool. Bring a large pan of water to boiling point, add the pineapple juice, salt and rice. Simmer for 12 minutes or until the rice is just tender. Drain it in a colander and rinse with cold water to remove the excess starch. Put the rice in a large bowl. Cut the chicken flesh into small pieces and add to the rice with the pineapple cubes, sultanas, raisins and onion. Pour boiling water over the mushrooms. Leave 5 minutes then drain them and slice thinly. Add to the rice mixture.

Mix together the sugar, salt, mustard and pepper for the dressing. Blend in the oil, then the vinegar. Stir the dressing into the rice mixture with a fork. Check the seasoning. Melt the butter in a pan and fry the almonds until they are golden brown. Put them on one side. Leave the chicken mixture, covered, in a cold place until it is needed. Just before serving blend in peas and scatter with the flaked almonds.

Ratatouille*

FOR 6

2 small aubergines; 2 courgettes; 8 tablespoons olive oil; 2 medium onions, finely sliced; 2 small green peppers, de-seeded and thinly sliced; 1 clove garlic, crushed; ½ lb. tomatoes, skinned, de-seeded and chopped; salt; pepper; 1 tablespoon chopped parsley

Preparation: 15 minutes *Cooking time: about 45 minutes*

Frozen ratatouille is well worth trying when these vegetables are expensive or buy ½ lb. courgettes and add them to frozen ratatouille as a spinner.

Cut the washed, unpeeled aubergines and courgettes in ½-in. cubes. Sprinkle with salt and leave them to drain on kitchen paper for about 30 minutes. Heat the olive oil in a large, heavy pan. Add the onions and cook them slowly until they are soft but not coloured. Dry the aubergines and courgettes on kitchen paper and add them to the pan with the green peppers and garlic. Cover and simmer very gently for 40 minutes, stirring occasionally so that the mixture does not stick to the pan. Add the tomatoes and plenty of seasoning.

Cover and cook for a further 30 minutes or until the vegetables are soft but still retain their shape. Stir in the parsley.

Serve hot as an accompanying vegetable or cold as an hors-d'oeuvre.

Duchess Potatoes

FOR 4

4-portion pack instant mashed potato; ½ oz. butter; 1 egg, beaten; salt; pepper

Preparation: 10 minutes *Cooking time: about 20 minutes*

Get out a baking tray.

Set oven at 400°F., Gas 6.

Make up the instant potato according to the directions on the packet. Blend in the butter and most of the egg, reserving about 1 teaspoon. Add salt and pepper to taste. Put the potato mixture into a large piping bag fitted with a large rose nozzle. Pipe the potato in whirls on the greased baking sheet. Leave in a cold place until required. Twenty minutes before serving blend 1 teaspoon water with the remaining egg, and use to glaze the potato whirls. Cook for 20 minutes or until heated through and golden brown.

Potatoes and Onions in Layers

FOR 6

2 lb. medium-sized potatoes, peeled; ½ lb. onions, peeled; salt; pepper

Preparation: 15 minutes *Cooking time: about 2 hours*

Get out a 2½-pint straight-sided oven-proof dish.

Set oven at 375°F., Gas 5.

Slice the potatoes and onions very thinly. Put them into a pan, cover with cold water, add 1 teaspoon salt and bring to boiling point. Boil 1 minute, then drain in a colander. Layer up potato and onion slices in the buttered dish, starting and finishing with a layer of potato. Season each layer with salt and pepper. Dot with the remaining butter. Bake for about 2 hours or until golden and tender. Add a little more butter during cooking if necessary.

Vichy Carrots in the Oven

FOR 6

1½ lb. carrots, scraped and sliced; ½ pint water; 1 oz. butter; 1½ level teaspoons caster sugar; salt; pepper

Preparation: 15 minutes *Cooking time: about 1½ hours*

Get out a 1½-pint oven-proof casserole.

Set oven at 350°F., Gas 4.

Put the carrots into the casserole. Add the water, butter, sugar and plenty of salt and pepper. Cover the casserole with a well-fitting lid or piece of foil and cook for about 1½ hours or until the carrots are tender.

Glazed Onions

FOR 4

1 oz. butter; 4 medium onions, peeled; salt; pepper

Preparation: 10 minutes *Cooking time: about 2 hours*

Get out a small, heavy, oven-proof casserole.

Set oven at 325°F., Gas 3.

Grease the bottom of the casserole with half the butter. Put the onions into the casserole and top each with a small piece of the remaining butter. Sprinkle the onions with a little salt and pepper, cover with a lid and cook for about 2 hours, or until tender.

Peas and Courgettes

FOR 4

½ lb. courgettes; salt; 12-oz. packet frozen peas, thawed; knob of butter

Preparation: 10 minutes *Cooking time: 5 minutes*

Top and tail the courgettes. Do not peel them. If they are very small cut them into ¼-in. thick slices. If they are larger cut them in cubes. Put them into a pan of boiling salted water with the peas. Cover and simmer about 5 minutes or until just tender. Drain thoroughly. Return to the pan and toss in butter over a low heat.

Buttered Peas and Cucumber

FOR 4

1 cucumber; salt; 2 oz. butter; 12-oz. packet frozen peas, thawed; pepper; sprig of mint; 1 teaspoon sugar; butter

Preparation: 10 minutes *Cooking time: about 10 minutes*

Peel the cucumber, cut it in 1-in. thick slices, then cut each slice in 1-in. long pencil-thick fingers. Sprinkle with salt and leave to drain on kitchen paper for about 15 minutes. Put the butter in a pan, add the cucumber, cover and cook gently for 5 minutes, stirring occasionally. Add the peas, salt and pepper to taste, and mint. Then add the sugar, cover and simmer for a further 5 minutes until the peas are cooked, shaking the pan from time to time. Remove mint before serving and toss in butter.

DESSERTS-CUM-PUDDINGS

Dutch Spiced Apple Tart*

FOR 6

Shortcrust pastry: 10 oz. plain flour; $\frac{1}{4}$ level teaspoon salt; $2\frac{1}{2}$ oz. butter; $2\frac{1}{2}$ oz. lard; about 10 teaspoons water

Filling: 1 lb. apples, peeled, cored and sliced; 4 oz. soft brown sugar; 2 oz. sultanas; 1 level teaspoon cinnamon; grated rind of half a lemon

Topping: About 1 tablespoon icing sugar

Preparation: 20 minutes *Cooking time: about 45 minutes*

Set oven at 425°F., Gas 7.

Get out a 7 × 11 in. Swiss roll tin and line it with greased greaseproof paper.

Make the shortcrust pastry in the usual way. Roll out a little more than half the pastry. Use to line the Swiss roll tin. Prick well with a fork. Roll out the remaining pastry to cover.

PREPARE THE FILLING: In a bowl mix together the apples, sugar, sultanas, cinnamon and lemon rind. Place this mixture over the pastry, moisten the edge of the pastry and cover with the pastry 'lid'. Press gently to seal the edges. Decorate the edges with a fork and make two slits in the top. Bake for 15 minutes at 425°F., Gas 7, then for about 30 minutes at 350°F., Gas 4. Lift carefully out of the tin, using the paper as a lever. Sprinkle with the icing sugar, cut into slices with a palette knife, lift each on to a serving dish and serve with lots of fresh cream.

When I first tasted this tart, it was served with brandy butter instead of cream, most extravagant but gorgeous!

French Apple Tart*

FOR 4

For the pastry: 4 oz. plain flour; pinch of salt; 1½ oz. butter; 1 oz. lard; 1 egg, separated; water

For the pastry cream: 1 egg; 1 oz. caster sugar; ½ oz. cornflour; ¼ pint milk; few drops vanilla essence

Filling: ½ lb. cooking apples, peeled, cored and very thinly sliced; ½–1 oz. caster sugar; ½ oz. butter, melted; 1 rounded tablespoon apricot jam; 1 tablespoon water

Preparation: 25 minutes *Cooking time: about 40 minutes*

Get out an 8- or 7-in. flan ring or tin.

Set oven at 400°F., Gas 6.

Start to make shortcrust pastry in the usual way until the fats and flour resemble fine breadcrumbs. Add the egg yolk with just enough water to mix to a firm dough. Roll out the pastry to about an 11-in. circle on a well-floured board. Line the flan ring with the pastry and prick the base well with a fork. Leave in the refrigerator or other cool place for 15 minutes to chill, then bake blind; place a piece of greaseproof paper in the flan case and fill with baking beans, or use crumpled foil, and bake for about 20 minutes. Remove the beans and paper 7 minutes or so before taking the flan case out of the oven when it is evenly and lightly browned.

Meanwhile prepare the pastry cream. Blend together the egg, sugar and cornflour and extra egg white left from pastry. Heat the milk to boiling point, pour on to the egg and flour mixture and stir briskly. Return to the pan and bring to boiling point. Simmer for 2–3 minutes, stirring all the time, until smooth and thick. Leave to cool slightly then add a few drops of vanilla essence.

When the flan case is cooked remove it from the oven. Fill the base of the case with the pastry cream. Arrange half the apples in the flan case, sprinkle with sugar, brush with butter. Put the remaining apples on top with the remaining sugar and butter. Bake at 350°F., Gas 4, for 15 minutes or until the apples are just soft. Remove the flan from the oven. Do not remove from the flan ring or tin.

Sieve the apricot jam into a bowl. Stir in the water and brush the top of the flan with this glaze. Leave to set. When cold remove the flan ring or tin and use the tart the same day. Serve cold.

Bakewell Tart*

FOR 4–6

For the shortcrust pastry: 6 oz. plain flour; ¼ level teaspoon salt; 1½ oz. butter; 1½ oz. lard; about 6 teaspoons cold water

For the filling: 1 heaped tablespoon raspberry or strawberry jam; 4 oz. butter; 4 oz. caster sugar; 1 egg; 4 oz. ground rice; ½ teaspoon almond essence

Preparation: 20 minutes *Cooking time: about 30 minutes*

Get out an 8-in. plain flan ring and a baking sheet.

Set oven at 400°F., Gas 6.

Make the shortcrust pastry in the usual way. Roll the pastry out thinly on a floured board. Use it to line the flan ring, which should be placed on the baking sheet. Prick the base of the flan case well with a fork then leave it in the refrigerator for 10 minutes.

Meanwhile prepare the filling. Heat the butter in a pan until it has just melted but is not brown. Stir in the sugar and cook for 1 minute then stir in the blended egg, ground rice and almond essence. Spread the jam in the base of the flan case and then pour the filling on top. Roll out the pastry trimmings and cut them into ¾-in. wide strips. Arrange them in a lattice on top of the pudding, making them stick with a little milk. Bake the pudding for about 30 minutes at 400°F., Gas 6 until it is well risen and golden brown. The filling should then spring back into shape when it is lightly pressed with the finger. Take tart out of oven and remove the flan ring. Leave to cool on a wire rack.

Lemon Meringue Pie*

FOR 4–6

Sweet shortcrust pastry: 6 oz. plain flour; pinch salt; 4 oz. butter; ½ oz. caster sugar; 1 egg yolk; 2 teaspoons water

Lemon filling: 2 large lemons; 1½ oz. cornflour; ½ pint water; 2 egg yolks; 3 oz. caster sugar
Meringue topping: 3 egg whites; 4½ oz. caster sugar

Preparation: 30 minutes *Total cooking time: 45 minutes*

Set oven at 400°F., Gas 6.

A must in every keen cook's recipe file. Takes time to make but well worth it.

FOR THE PASTRY: Sift the flour and salt into a bowl. Cut the butter in small pieces then rub it into the flour with the fingertips until the mixture resembles fine breadcrumbs. Mix the egg yolk, sugar and water together, add to the dry ingredients and bind together, kneading lightly. Roll out the pastry on a lightly floured, cool surface to a circle approximately 10 in. in diameter and use to line the flan ring, which should be placed on a reversed baking tray. If time allows, let it rest in the refrigerator for 20 minutes or so before baking.

TO BAKE: Fill the uncooked flan case with a crumpled piece of kitchen foil, or greaseproof paper and baking beans to keep the shape. Bake with oven at 400°F., Gas 6 for 15 minutes. Then remove the foil, or greaseproof paper and baking beans, and bake for a further 5 to 10 minutes to dry out the centre. Remove the flan case from the oven, cool, then remove the flan ring.

TO MAKE THE FILLING: Finely grate the lemon rind, squeeze out the juice and put both in a bowl with the cornflour. Add 2 tablespoons of the water and blend together to form a smooth paste. Boil the remaining water and pour it on to the cornflour mixture, stirring briskly. Return all the mixture to the pan, bring to boiling point, stirring all the time, and simmer for 3 minutes. Remove the pan from the heat and add the egg yolks blended with the sugar. Cool slightly, then spoon the filling into the flan case and put it to one side.

TO MAKE THE MERINGUE TOPPING: Whisk the egg whites with a rotary whisk until they will form stiff peaks, then add the sugar a teaspoon at a time, whisking well after each addition, until all the sugar has been incorporated. Spoon the meringue over the lemon filling, being careful to cover up to the edge of the pastry and leaving no air spaces.

Return the pie to the oven, (350°F., Gas 4) for 15 minutes. Serve warm or cold.

French Apricot Flan* FOR THE GRAND OCCASION

FOR 12

For the flan case: 12 oz. plain flour; ¼ level teaspoon salt; 1 level tablespoon icing sugar; 4 oz. butter; 3 oz. lard; about 9 teaspoons water

Confectioner's custard: 3 eggs; 3 oz. caster sugar; 1½ oz. flour; ¾ pint milk; vanilla essence

Fruit filling: 1-lb. 13-oz. can and 15-oz. can apricot halves

Arrowroot glaze: 3 level teaspoons arrowroot; ½ pint fruit juice; 2 tablespoons apricot brandy

Preparation: 30 minutes *Total cooking time: 30 minutes*

Get out an 11-in. shallow fluted flan tin with a removable base.

Set oven at 400°F., Gas 6.

Sift the flour and salt into a bowl. Add the icing sugar. Cut the fats in small pieces then rub them into the flour until the mixture resembles fine breadcrumbs. Add enough water to make a firm dough. Roll the pastry out on a lightly floured board and use to line the flan tin. Fill with greaseproof paper and baking beans or foil. Leave in a cold place for 15 minutes then bake in the pre-heated oven for 25 minutes. Remove the paper, beans or foil and bake for a further 5 minutes to dry the base of the flan case.

Remove the flan from the oven and leave it to cool.

Blend together the eggs and sugar for the confectioner's custard. Add the flour and a little of the milk to make a smooth paste. Boil the remaining milk. Pour it on to the egg mixture. Stir well then return it to the pan. Bring to the boil, stirring, and simmer 2 or 3 minutes until thick. Remove from the heat and stir frequently so that a skin does not form. Add the vanilla essence. When the custard is cold spread it in the base of the flan case.

Drain the apricots. Arrange them on top of the custard. Put the arrowroot in a pan. Slowly blend in the apricot juice. Bring to the boil and simmer until thick. Stir in the apricot brandy. Spoon or brush the glaze over the fruit. Leave in a cool place until set.

Pancakes

MAKES ABOUT 10 PANCAKES

4 oz. plain flour; pinch salt; 2 eggs; just under ½ pint milk and water mixed; salad oil

Preparation: 20 minutes *Cooking time: about 20 minutes*

Get out a 7-in. heavy based frying-pan.

This recipe for pancake batter has one more egg than usual which makes a richer batter which is easier to handle.

Sift the flour and salt into a bowl. Make a well in the centre of the flour and blend in the eggs with a little of the milk, using a small wire whisk, to make a smooth paste. Blend in enough of the remaining milk to make a batter the consistency of double cream. Beat it well.

Heat about 2 tablespoons salad oil in the frying-pan, drain off as much oil as possible, then pour in just enough batter to cover the bottom of the pan thinly. Cook until the pancake is pale golden brown, then turn it and cook it on the other side. Turn out on sugared greaseproof paper. To keep hot, layer up between two plates and leave in a cool oven until needed. Use up the remaining batter in the same way.

Serve with lemon wedges and caster sugar. Alternatively each pancake may be stuffed with a fruit purée such as apricot or apple and mincemeat and then rolled up, sprinkled with sugar and crisped in the oven.

Super Dairy Ice-Cream—No cooking*

FOR 8

4 eggs, separated; 4 oz. icing sugar, sifted; ½ pint double cream; flavouring (see below)

Preparation: 20 minutes

Get out one shallow 2½-pint or two shallow 1¼-pint plastic refrigerator containers with lids.

Set your refrigerator to the coldest setting, following your refrigerator manufacturer's instructions.

This ice-cream is fabulous. If your ice-cream freezing compartment doesn't freeze very quickly freeze the ice-cream in a shallow container so that it has more contact with the actual freezing surface.

Whisk the egg yolks with a small wire whisk in a small bowl until they are well blended.

In another, larger bowl (about 3 pint) whisk the egg whites with a balloon or rotary whisk until they form stiff peaks, then beat in the sugar a teaspoon at a time until it has all been included.

Slowly whisk the blended egg yolks with the white meringue mixture. Lightly whip the cream until it is frothy and will form soft peaks, then fold it into the egg mixture.

Add any flavouring required, see below, mixing it in thoroughly, then turn the ice-cream into the plastic container and cover it with a lid. This will make it keep more satisfactorily if your refrigerator freezing compartment is big enough to take the container. If not, use a freezer tray and cover it with a lid of foil. Leave the ice-cream in the freezer compartment for at least 4 hours to set before serving. If you have a deep freeze it will set quicker, of course.

VARIATIONS OF THE BASIC THEME

Vanilla ice-cream: add ½ teaspoon vanilla essence to the whipped cream before folding it into the egg mixture.

Mint ice-cream: add a few drops of oil of peppermint and a little green colouring to the mixture just before putting it into the freezer tray. When serving, decorate with fresh mint if available.

Coffee and Rum ice-cream: add 2 tablespoons coffee essence and a tablespoon rum to the mixture before putting it into the freezer tray.

Chocolate ice-cream: blend 2 oz. drinking chocolate with the egg yolks, then finish as for the basic recipe.

Raspberry or Strawberry ice-cream: sieve 8 oz. fresh or thawed frozen fruit and fold it into the mixture with a few drops of red colouring before putting it into the freezer container.

Rum and Raisin ice-cream: soak 4 oz. plump, halved, seedless raisins in a bowl with 4 tablespoons rum for half an hour. Fold into the mixture before putting it into the freezer container. Freeze until nearly set, then see note below.

Tutti Frutti ice-cream: soak 4 oz. chopped glacé fruits in 3 tablespoons kirsch or brandy for half an hour. Fold into the mixture before putting it into the freezer container. Freeze until nearly set, then see note below.

Pineapple and Cherry crush ice-cream: finely chop 12 maraschino cherries and 4 rings fresh or canned pineapple. Fold into the mixture together with a few drops of yellow colouring and 1 tablespoon maraschino from the cherries.

Note: When making the last three variations a better result will be obtained by freezing the mixture until it is almost set, then turning it into a bowl, stirring it thoroughly to distribute the fruit evenly in the mixture and returning it to the freezer tray.

Fruity Ice-Cream—Using Bought Ice-Cream*

FOR 4

2 oz. seedless raisins, chopped; 2 oz. walnuts, chopped; 2 oz. glacé cherries, chopped; 3 tablespoons orange liqueur to taste; 17-oz. block vanilla Dairy ice-cream

Preparation: 10 minutes

When you haven't time to make your own ice-cream, try this.

Plump up the raisins in a bowl of hot water for ten minutes then drain them thoroughly, chop them and put them into a bowl with the walnuts, cherries, and orange liqueur. Put the ice-cream into another bowl and mix it until it is soft. Stir in the contents of the first bowl and mix it until it is soft and well blended. Put the ice-cream into a freezing tray and leave it to freeze overnight. Scoop it out and serve with ice-cream wafers.

Syllabub*

FOR THE GRAND OCCASION

FOR 4

1 large lemon; ¼ pint fairly sweet sherry; 2 tablespoons brandy; 2 oz. caster sugar; ½ pint double cream

Preparation: 10 minutes

Simplicity itself and very rich.

Finely grate the lemon rind and squeeze out the juice. Put the rind and juice in a bowl with the sherry, brandy and sugar. Stir until the sugar has dissolved. Pour in the cream and whisk the mixture until it will form soft peaks when the whisk is lifted out.

Spoon into 4 individual glasses and leave in a cool place until required. Serve with cats' tongues or boudoir biscuits.

Hot Lemon Soufflé

FOR 4

1½ oz. butter; 1½ oz. flour; ½ pint milk; 1½ oz. caster sugar; grated rind and juice of one large lemon; 3 eggs, separated

Preparation: 15 minutes *Cooking time: 35 minutes*

Get out a 2-pint soufflé dish.

Who wants to be in the kitchen just before dinner making the soufflé from start to finish—no one, so for a hot soufflé make as far as the sauce plus yolk stage beforehand, then 40 minutes before serving, just whisk the egg whites and fold into the prepared sauce.

Butter a 2-pint soufflé dish. Melt the butter in a pan, blend in the flour and cook over a low heat for one minute without browning. Stir in the milk a little at a time so that no lumps form. Bring to the boil and simmer until thickened. Stir in the sugar, lemon rind and lemon juice. Remove from the heat and stir in the egg yolks one at a time. Whisk the whites until stiff and fold into the mixture. Turn it into the prepared dish and bake at 350°F., Gas 4 for 35 minutes or until the top is firm to the touch and the soufflé is well risen. Serve at once.

Chilled Lemon Flan*

FOR 4, OR 6 AT A PINCH

For the flan case: 4 oz. digestive biscuits; 1 oz. caster sugar; 2 oz. butter, melted

For the lemon filling: 2 individual portions lemon mousse, the frozen variety, defrosted; finely grated rind and juice of 1 large

lemon; 3 oz. caster sugar; ¼ pint double cream, lightly whipped
For decoration: 5 thin lemon slices

Preparation: 15 minutes

Get out a 7-in. plain flan ring and a flat serving plate.

This delicious tart/biscuit crust/flan has a filling which is a cross between an ice-cream and a mousse.

Put the digestive biscuits between two pieces of greaseproof paper on a wooden board and crush them with a rolling-pin to form fine crumbs. Put these crumbs into a bowl with the sugar. Stir in the butter and mix it in thoroughly. Put the flan on to the plate and then spoon the biscuit crumb mixture into it. Using the back of a tablespoon press the crumbs against the sides of the flan ring and on to the plate to form a flan case. Put the flan into the refrigerator to chill. A flan ring and plate are used so that you can use your favourite plate without any turning out difficulties—just lift off the ring.

Meanwhile prepare the filling. Put the mousse into a bowl, add the lemon rind and juice and mash with a fork until the mixture is smooth. Stir in the sugar and cream then pour the lemon filling into the flan case. Put the flan into the *freezing compartment* of your refrigerator and leave it to set for at least an hour before serving.

Just before serving decorate the flan with the slices of lemon or with crystallized lemon slices, or grated chocolate. If the flan is made, say, a day in advance, it will be quite frozen so lift it into the ordinary part of the refrigerator about 1½ hours before serving.

Chilled Dessert Cheesecake*

FOR 6

12 oz. cottage cheese; ¼ pint single cream; ¾ oz. powdered gelatine; 4 tablespoons cold water; juice and finely grated rind of two large lemons; 3 standard eggs, separated; 4 oz. caster sugar; ¼ pint double cream, lightly whipped
For decoration: fresh strawberries or raspberries or canned apricots, peaches, oranges or cherries, well drained of juice; sieved apricot jam
Crust: 8 digestive biscuits, crushed with a rolling-pin; 1 oz. demerara sugar; 2 oz. butter, melted

Preparation: 30 minutes

Get out an 8-in. cake tin or soufflé dish.

In America these are made in spring moulds which means the sides of the tin are loose and you don't therefore have to turn the cheesecake out. A cake tin works very well with the crumbs put on top so that once turned out the crumbs are underneath.

Lightly butter an 8-in. cake tin or soufflé dish and carefully line with ungreased greaseproof paper, the sides first, then a circle of paper in the bottom.

Sieve the cottage cheese into a large bowl or pulp in the blender, and blend in single cream. Soften the gelatine in a basin with the water for five minutes then place basin over a pan of simmering water, making sure that the water does not touch the bottom of the bowl, until the gelatine is dissolved.

Put the lemon juice and rind with the egg yolks and sugar in a large bowl and stand it over a pan of simmering water. Whisk until thick and foamy, remove from the heat and whisk until cool.

Blend together the egg yolk mixture, gelatine and cottage cheese. When thick but not set fold in the whisked egg whites and lightly whipped double cream, saving 2 tablespoons for decoration. Turn it into the prepared tin. Chill in refrigerator until set.

Combine the crust ingredients in a bowl, mix well with a fork. Sprinkle over the cheesecake mixture, press down lightly. Chill until firm. Turn out carefully on to a 9 to 10-in. plate, peel off the paper, releasing with the blade of a knife. Decorate with fruit all over the top, then brush with sieved apricot jam mixed with a little warm water.

Chilled Apricot Soufflé* FOR THE GRAND OCCASION

FOR 6

1 lb. fresh apricots; 1 tablespoon water; 2 oz. caster sugar; thinly peeled rind of ½ a lemon; 3 large eggs, separated; 3 oz. caster sugar; juice of ½ a lemon; ½ oz. powdered gelatine (1 packet); 3 tablespoons cold water; ¼ pint double cream; ¼ pint single cream; 1 tablespoon apricot brandy or brandy

Preparation: 30 minutes

Get out a 1- to $1\frac{1}{4}$-pint capacity soufflé dish.

Vary this from time to time by using other fruits in season; raspberries and strawberries don't need cooking beforehand. Gooseberries make a good one—add a dash of green colouring to give a pleasing colour.

First prepare the soufflé dish.

Measure a piece of greaseproof paper large enough to go round the outside of the soufflé dish and three times as deep as the dish. Fold the paper in half lengthways then fold over a $\frac{1}{2}$-in. strip along the folded edge. Put the paper round the dish with the $\frac{1}{2}$-in. strip inside and at the base of the dish. Secure the top of the paper collar with a paper-clip and then tie a piece of string firmly round the dish or use Sellotape to seal the join.

Put the apricots in a pan with the water, lemon peel and sugar. Cover the pan with a well-fitting lid and gently simmer the apricots until they are tender.

Remove the lemon peel, cut the apricots in half and remove the stones then work the pulp through a sieve. (You should have about $\frac{1}{2}$ pint apricot purée.) Put the gelatine and water into a small bowl over a pan of hot, not boiling water and leave it to dissolve, stirring from time to time. Put the egg yolks, caster sugar and lemon juice into a fairly large bowl. Place the bowl over a pan of hot water and with a rotary or balloon whisk, whisk the mixture until it is thick and pale in colour.

Remove the bowl from the heat and whisk in the apricot purée. Blend in the dissolved gelatine and the apricot brandy, mixing thoroughly, then leave the mixture in a cold place, stirring occasionally, until it has thickened but not set.

Meanwhile whip the two creams together until they will just form soft peaks, but be careful not to overwhip the cream. Fold the cream into the thickened apricot mixture, reserving a little for decoration. Whisk the egg whites until they form soft peaks and fold them into the mixture. Pour the soufflé into the prepared dish and leave it in a cool place to set—preferably overnight.

Before serving remove the paper very carefully by working it away from the sides of the soufflé with the back of a knife. Decorate the top of the soufflé with cream.

Ginger Biscuit Cream Roll*

FOR 4

½ pint double cream; ½ lb. ginger biscuits; crystallized ginger.

Preparation: 10 minutes

This is a great standby of mine when the 'phone goes and I've people coming for dinner the next day. I get a packet of ginger biscuits out of the store cupboard and sandwich them together with a can of cream—I usually haven't spare double cream on hand. Then the next day I mask the whole thing over with ¼ pint freshly-whipped double cream, decorate it with ginger and Bob's your uncle!

Put half the cream into a bowl and whisk until the mixture forms fairly stiff peaks. Use this to sandwich the ginger biscuits together in a long sausage shaped roll. Arrange on a serving dish and leave in the refrigerator or other cool place overnight. Whisk the remaining cream the next day and cover the ginger biscuit roll completely with cream. Decorate with small pieces or slices of crystallized ginger.

Cut into diagonal slices to serve, which gives a stripey effect.

Peach Condé*

FOR 4–6

2½-oz. carton double cream; 15-oz. can creamed rice; 15-oz. can halved peaches; strawberry jam; cherry brandy or kirsch

Preparation: 10 minutes

If you've a can of creamed rice, some canned fruit such as peaches, apricots, or cherries and some strawberry jam in the cupboard you can whizz this up in a trice.

Whisk the cream until it forms soft peaks. Turn the creamed rice into a bowl then fold in the cream. Divide the mixture between 4 or 6 individual glasses and put to chill in the refrigerator or other cool place.

Drain the peaches, or other fruit, arrange on top of creamed rice. Spoon over strawberry jam thinned down with a soupçon of cherry brandy or what you can glean from the drinks cupboard.

Pots au Chocolat* FOR THE GRAND OCCASION

FOR 4

6 oz. plain chocolate; ½ oz. butter; 3 eggs, separated; 1 tablespoon rum; 1 tablespoon coffee essence; 4 teaspoons whipped cream

Preparation: 15 minutes

Use small ramekins or the smallest coffee cups to serve this dessert in.

Put the chocolate and butter in a bowl and place the bowl over a pan of hot, not boiling water. Leave the chocolate to dissolve, stirring occasionally. Remove it from the heat and beat in the egg yolks, rum and coffee essence. Whisk the egg whites until they are stiff and then fold them into the mixture. Pour it into four small ramekins or coffee cups and leave in a cool place until set.

Just before serving top each with cream and a sprinkling of grated chocolate.

Orange Sorbet*

FOR 4

3 oz. caster sugar; ½ pint water; 6 fl. oz. can concentrated frozen orange juice, undiluted; 1 egg white, whisked stiffly

Preparation: 20 minutes

No oranges to squeeze for this one! Take one can of the frozen orange juice. Set your refrigerator to the coldest setting following the manufacturer's instructions.

Put the sugar and water in a pan and heat slowly until the sugar has dissolved. Allow this syrup to cool. Add the orange juice to the sugar syrup, blend together, then pour it into a 1-pint, preferably shallow, plastic-lidded container. Freeze the sorbet for half an hour, or until it is barely firm. Turn it into a bowl and mash it down until there are no large pieces, then fold in the stiffly whisked egg white, put the lid on, return the sorbet to the freezer compartment until it is required.

To serve, scoop out spoonfuls into individual chilled glasses, top with mint or fresh orange slices.

Crème Brulée*

FOR THE GRAND OCCASION

FOR 6

4 egg yolks; 2 oz. caster sugar; ½ pint double cream; ½ pint single cream; vanilla essence; extra caster sugar for topping

Preparation: 20 minutes *Cooking time: 45 minutes*

Get out a 1½-pint deep oven-proof dish—a soufflé dish is ideal.
Set oven at 275°F., Gas 1.
A rich classic cream custard.

Beat the egg yolks with the sugar until they are well blended. Put the two creams into a pan and bring them just to simmering point. Pour the cream on to the egg yolks and stir well. Return the custard to the pan and cook it over a very low heat, stirring all the time. The custard must not be allowed even to simmer or it will curdle. When the custard is thick enough to coat the back of a wooden spoon stir in a few drops of vanilla essence and then strain the custard into the dish. Stand the dish in a meat tin containing 1 in. of warm water and bake the custard for about 45 minutes or until it is just firm. Remove the dish from the oven, leave the custard to cool then put the dish into the refrigerator or other cold place for several hours or overnight. Next day sprinkle the surface of the custard generously with caster sugar so that it is completely covered. Heat the grill and put the dish under it. Leave it to melt slowly so that the sugar forms a caramel. Remove the dish from the heat and leave it to stand for a further 2 or 3 hours in a cold place before serving.

Marinaded Oranges*

FOR 6

8 thin-skinned oranges; 4 oz. caster sugar; 4 tablespoons Cointreau, Grand Marnier or Curaçao (or more to taste)

Preparation: 15 minutes

Peel the oranges with a small sharp knife so that all the peel and pith is removed. Divide the oranges into segments, removing as much of the membrane between each segment as possible or, if you are in a hurry, cut into slices. Put the orange segments into the dish and then mix in the caster sugar. Add the liqueur and put the dish into the refrigerator or other cold place for at least an hour before serving.

Serve chilled with crisp, thin biscuits such as cats' tongues.

Old-Fashioned Sherry Trifle* FOR THE GRAND OCCASION

FOR 6

6 small sponge cakes; plenty of strawberry jam; 2 oz. ratafia biscuits, or broken macaroons; 10 tablespoons sherry, or sherry and fruit juice; 8 maraschino cherries, chopped; 1 tablespoon juice from bottle of cherries

For the custard: 2 egg yolks; 1 oz. caster sugar; ½ pint milk

For decoration: ½ pint double cream; ½ oz. blanched, split almonds, lightly toasted under the grill

Preparation: 20 minutes

You will need a 2-pint shallow glass serving dish.

This is the real thing, extravagant yes, but such a joy to eat. If you haven't time to make egg custard make ½ pint fairly thick packet custard and beat really well with a rotary or wire whisk, adding a little of the top of the milk.

Split the sponge cakes in half, then sandwich them together with strawberry jam. Arrange the cakes in the base of the dish and sprinkle the ratafia biscuits in between them. Sprinkle first the sherry, then the cherries and maraschino juice, over the sponge cakes and biscuits.

TO MAKE THE CUSTARD: Blend the egg yolks and sugar very thoroughly in a bowl. Heat the milk to simmering point and pour it on to the egg yolks. Stir the mixture well, then return the custard to the pan and cook it over a very low heat—it must not boil at all or it will curdle—until it is thick enough to coat the back of a wooden spoon. Leave it to cool, then strain it over the sponge cakes and leave it to set.

Just before serving, whip the cream until it is thick enough to form soft peaks, then spread it over the trifle. Spike the top with lightly toasted almonds.

Fresh Pineapple and Fruit Salad*

FOR 10

1 large pineapple; 1 small melon; 1 eating apple; ½ lb. pears; 4-oz. jar Maraschino cherries; a few canned or fresh white grapes; caster sugar; 2 tablespoons Grand Marnier or Cointreau liqueur; ½ to ¾ pint double fresh cream for serving

Preparation: 15 minutes

A fresh pineapple cut in half lengthways giving two spectacular shells to fill with fruit salad—splendid for a help-yourself dessert table.

Leave all the green top on and cut the pineapple in half lengthways. Cut out the flesh, using a grapefruit knife. Remove the core, cut the flesh into small pieces, and place in a bowl with the melon, cut in small cubes. Peel, core and slice the apple and pears. Add them to the fruit in the bowl with the drained cherries and skinned and pipped grapes. Sprinkle the fruit with caster sugar to taste, and add the liqueur. Leave the bowl, covered, until the sugar has dissolved. Then pile the fruit back into the pineapple shells. The remaining fruit salad may be offered separately. Serve with thin biscuits and cream.

Baked Meringue with Chestnut Cream FOR THE GRAND OCCASION

FOR 8

For the meringue base: 3 egg whites; 6 oz. caster sugar; ½ oz. browned shredded almonds

For the filling: 8¾-oz. tin sweetened chestnut purée; ½ pint double cream; 1–2 tablespoons sherry

Preparation: 20 minutes *Cooking time: about 2–3 hours*

Get out a baking sheet lined with non-stick household parchment or well greased greaseproof.

Set oven at 225°F., Gas ¼.

Baked meringue topped with a thick chestnut cream. Make the meringue well beforehand then assemble half an hour before it is required.

Beat the egg whites until they are really stiff then whisk in a level dessertspoonful of the sugar. Continue to whisk until the sugar is well blended then add the remaining sugar in the same way, a dessertspoon at a time.

Have ready the baking sheet, lined, on which has been drawn an 8-in. circle. Spread the meringue to fill the circle, smooth it with a palette knife, sprinkle the almonds all round the edge. Bake the meringue for 2–3 hours or until crisp.

Remove the meringue from the oven and leave to cool on a wire rack. (If stored in foil or an airtight tin the meringue will keep for several weeks until required.)

Put the chestnut purée into a bowl. In another bowl whip the cream until it will just form soft peaks—be very careful not to over-whip it. Fold the cream into the purée with the sherry. Pile the filling on to the meringue base. Decorate with marrons glacé or more cream if liked.

Baked Cherry Meringue

FOR 8

Make the meringue 8-in. base as in the previous recipe, hollow out the centre a little before baking. When baked and cool and half an hour before serving, spread with ½ pint whipped cream and spoon the contents of a tin of cherry pie filling on top.

Raspberry Meringue FOR THE GRAND OCCASION

FOR 6

Meringue case: 4 egg whites; 8 oz. caster sugar; ½ oz. flaked or shredded, blanched almonds
Filling: ½ pint double cream; 1 oz. caster sugar; 2 teaspoons brandy or a few drops of vanilla essence; ½–1 lb. raspberries

Preparation: 25 minutes *Cooking time: about 3 hours*

Set oven at 225°F., Gas ¼.

Line two large baking trays with non-stick household parchment or well-greased greaseproof. On the paper on one baking sheet mark out a circle 8½ in. in diameter. On the other mark one 7½ in. and another 5½ in. in diameter. Use plates and saucer as guides.

Separate the egg yolks from the whites very carefully. Whisk the whites with a rotary whisk until they form soft peaks. Then add the sugar in level tablespoonfuls, whisking the mixture well after each addition. Continue in this way until all but a dessertspoonful of the sugar has been included; the sugar may be added a little more quickly during the latter part of the whisking.

Divide the mixture and spread it to cover the marked circles, smooth it with a knife to level off the surface, and, on the smallest circle, lift up the meringue in peaks then sprinkle it with remaining sugar and the almonds. Bake the meringue on the lower shelves of a very cool oven, 225°F., Gas ¼, for 3 to 4 hours.

When the meringue layers are completely firm to the touch, remove them from the oven, leave them to cool, then peel off the paper and store them, wrapped in foil or in a polythene bag or in a large cake tin, until they are required—they can be made days beforehand. 1½ hours before serving, lightly whip cream, add the sugar and brandy or vanilla and blend the cream with the raspberries. Spread half the mixture on lower layer, the rest on second layer and assemble cake in layers. The meringue will soften slightly before it is served. For a crisper meringue, assemble the cake only half an hour before serving.

Caramel Custard*

FOR 4

For the caramel: 3 oz. granulated sugar; 3 tablespoons water
For the custard: 4 eggs; 1 pint milk; 1½ oz. caster sugar; few drops vanilla essence

Preparation: 15 minutes *Cooking time: about 1¼ hours*

Get out a 1½-pint charlotte mould or cake tin; a meat tin.

Set the oven at 325°F., Gas 3.

Prepare the caramel. Put the sugar into a heavy pan with the water and leave it to dissolve over a gentle heat without boiling. When it has dissolved bring the syrup to boiling point and boil it until it is golden brown, then pour it into the charlotte mould or cake tin and swirl it round the base and sides.

Blend the eggs together in a bowl. Warm the milk in a pan, then pour it on to the eggs, mixing well. Blend in the sugar and vanilla essence. Strain the custard into the mould then place the mould in the meat tin, which should be half filled with hot water. Place it on the bottom shelf of the oven and bake the custard for 1¼ hours, or until the centre is just firm to the touch. It may take longer, depending on your oven, but this does not matter as long as the custard is not allowed to boil, which would cause it to curdle. Remove the custard from the oven and leave it in a cold place overnight before turning it out on to a flat serving dish.

Savarin au Rhum* — FOR THE GRAND OCCASION

FOR 12

¼ pint plus 5 tablespoons milk; 1 level teaspoon caster sugar; 2½ level teaspoons dried yeast; 12 oz. plain flour; pinch of salt; 3 eggs, beaten; 4½ oz. butter, melted

For the Rum Syrup: 1¼ lb. granulated sugar; 1 pint of water; 6 to 10 tablespoons rum

For the Apricot Glaze: 3 rounded tablespoons apricot jam; 1 tablespoon water

For the Filling: a selection of fruits in season; about 2 lb. prepared fruit, e.g. sliced apple, pear, banana, peach, apricot, nectarine, orange, grapes

Preparation: 35 minutes *Cooking time: about 40 minutes*

Get out a 9-inch (3-pint) oven-proof ring mould, well brushed with melted lard.

Set the oven at 425°F., Gas 7.

Heat the milk over a low heat until it is just warm, then turn it into a small bowl, stir in the sugar and whisk in the dried yeast with a fork. Leave the bowl in a warm place for about 10 minutes until mixture is frothy.

Sift the flour and the salt into a large mixing bowl. Make a hollow in the flour, pour in the yeast mixture and the beaten eggs and mix with a wooden spoon to a smooth dough. Then beat in the melted and cooled butter with the hand. Continue to beat the dough for a few minutes by hand until it is really smooth.

Turn the prepared dough into the greased ring mould. It will be the consistency of a thick batter and should be spread evenly in the mould. Cover the mould with a polythene bag and leave it in a warm place for about 30 to 40 minutes, or until the dough has risen almost to the top of the mould.

Bake the savarin in the pre-heated oven for about 25 minutes until it is deep golden brown and feels firm to the touch. Leave the savarin to cool in the tin for 5 minutes or so then turn it out on to a wire rack and place the rack over a large plate or a tray.

While the savarin is cooking, prepare the rum syrup. Put the sugar into a heavy-based pan with the water and dissolve it over a very gentle heat without allowing it to simmer at all. When the sugar has dissolved completely, bring the syrup up to boiling point and boil it for 1 minute, then remove the saucepan from the heat and stir in all the rum.

Using a very fine skewer or a darning needle, make holes all over the top of the savarin on the wire rack, then spoon the rum syrup over it so that it is absorbed by the warm savarin. When all the syrup in the pan has been used, pour any syrup which has drained on to the plate or tray back into the pan and coat the savarin again. Continue in this way until about ¼ pint of the syrup is left. Save this for the fruit salad. Transfer the savarin to a serving plate.

Sieve the apricot jam into a bowl, blend in the water and brush the surface of the savarin with this glaze to make it shiny.

Prepare the fresh fruit salad, add the remaining rum syrup to some of it and use this to fill centre of savarin. Arrange the rest of the fruit salad round the top and the outside of the savarin.

Serve with whipped cream.

Queen of Puddings

FOR 6

3 slices de-crusted white bread (3 oz.); ¾ pint milk; 3 eggs, separated; 7½ oz. caster sugar; finely grated rind of 1 lemon; 1 oz. butter; 3 level tablespoons strawberry or raspberry jam

Preparation: 20 minutes *Total cooking time: about 40 minutes*

Get out a 2½-pint shallow oven-proof dish.

Set oven at 325°F., Gas 3.

Put the bread into a bowl with half of the milk, and mash it with a fork until it is smooth. Stir in the egg yolks, 1½ oz. of the sugar, the lemon rind and the rest of the milk. Pour the mixture into the dish and dot it with the butter, cut into very small pieces. Bake it for about 30 minutes (325°F., Gas 3), or until the pudding is just set.

Remove from the oven and increase the oven temperature to 400°F., Gas 6. Spread the pudding with the jam.

Whisk the egg whites until they form soft peaks. Add the rest of the sugar a teaspoon at a time, whisking well after each addition. When all the sugar has been added pile the meringue on top of the pudding. Return it to the oven and bake it for 10 minutes or until the meringue has turned pale brown.

Nougat Pudding*

FOR 4

6-oz. can evaporated milk; 1 oz. glacé cherries; 2 oz. marshmallows; ½ lemon jelly tablet; ¼ pint very hot water; juice of ½ lemon; 1 oz. caster sugar; cream to decorate

Preparation: 20 minutes

Get out 4 individual glass serving dishes.

Chill the evaporated milk in the refrigerator. Chop the cherries finely. Cut the marshmallows in small pieces with wet scissors. Dissolve the jelly in the hot water. Cool the jelly until it is thick but not set. Whip the evaporated milk until it is light and foamy. Add the cooled jelly, blending it in well. Stir in the lemon juice, cherries, marshmallows and sugar. Turn into the individual bowls and chill.

Serve decorated with whipped cream.

Apple Jalousie*

MAKES 6–8 SLICES

For the filling: 1 lb. cooking apples, peeled, cored and sliced; 2 tablespoons water; 1 oz. butter; 2 oz. granulated sugar

For the pastry case: 11-oz. packet frozen puff pastry, thawed; 1 egg white, beaten.

Preparation: 15 minutes *Cooking time: about 25 minutes*

Get out a baking tray. Set oven at 400°F., Gas 6.

Put the apple slices into a pan with the water, butter and sugar. Cover the pan and simmer the apples until they are tender. Remove the lid and continue to cook the apples, mashing them with a wooden spoon as they simmer. Cook until the apple is a thick purée. Cool.

When the pastry has thawed, roll it out on a lightly floured board to a rectangle 8 by 12 in., then cut it into two strips each 4 by 12 in. Lay one strip on the baking tray, brush round the edge with beaten egg white then spoon the cold apple down the centre. Fold the second strip in half lengthways and cut with a sharp knife across the fold at 2-in. intervals, leaving 1 in. of pastry uncut at the sides. Unfold and place strip on top of the filling and press it on firmly. Knock up the edges with the back of a knife and brush the top with beaten egg white. Bake in the pre-heated oven for 25 minutes, or until it is well risen and golden. Remove it from the oven and brush again with egg white. Serve it hot as a pudding or cold for tea.

Christmas Pudding*

MAKES 1 LARGE AND 2 SMALL PUDDINGS

8 oz. self-raising flour; 1 level teaspoon mixed spice; ½ level teaspoon grated nutmeg; 1 level teaspoon salt; 1 lb. currants; 1 lb. sultanas; 1 lb. stoned raisins: ¾ lb. fresh white breadcrumbs; ¾ lb. suet, finely chopped; 4 oz. candied peel, finely chopped; 2 oz. almonds, blanched and chopped; 1 cooking apple, peeled, cored and grated; grated rind and juice of 1 orange; 1 lb. soft brown sugar; 6 eggs, beaten; ¼ pint stout

Preparation: 20 minutes *Cooking time: 6–8 hours*

Get out one 2½-pint and two 1½-pint pudding basins.

Sift together the flour, mixed spice, nutmeg and salt. Wash and dry currants, sultanas and raisins as above. Put breadcrumbs, suet, peel, almonds, grated apple, orange rind and juice into a large bowl. Stir in the spiced flour, dried fruit and sugar. Finally add the eggs and stout. Stir the mixture well, then turn into the greased basins, cover the tops with greaseproof paper and a foil lid, and let the puddings simmer gently for 6 to 8 hours. Lift them out of the pans, leaving the foil and greaseproof in place. Cool and store the puddings. Let them simmer for 3 hours before serving.

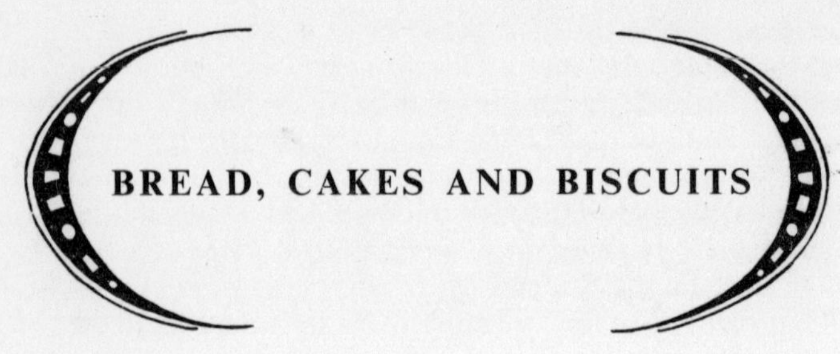

BREAD, CAKES AND BISCUITS

BREADMAKING

To get the finest results it is best to choose a strong plain flour blended especially for baking white bread and yeast recipes as it absorbs liquid easily and develops quickly, with kneading, into a firm, elastic dough. If strong flour is not available use good quality plain flour.

White Bread

This method of making white bread (sufficient for four small loaves) may be used as a basis for simpler types of yeast cookery.

Dough: 3 lb. plain flour; 1 oz. salt (2 level tablespoons); 1 oz. lard, rubbed in; 1 pint water (less 3 tablespoons)
Yeast liquid: Blend 1 oz. fresh yeast in $\frac{1}{2}$ pint water; or dissolve 1 teaspoon sugar in $\frac{1}{2}$ pint warm (110°F.) water, sprinkle 1 level tablespoon dried yeast on top, and leave until frothy—about 10 minutes.

Preparation: 25 minutes *Cooking time: about 40 minutes*

MIXING: Blend dry ingredients in a large bowl with yeast liquid, lard and water. Work to a firm dough, adding extra flour if needed, until the dough leaves the bowl clean. (You may need a little more flour or water to make the dough, depending on the type of flour used.) Turn the dough on to a lightly floured board and knead until it feels firm and elastic and no longer sticky—about 10 minutes. Shape the kneaded dough into a round ball, place in a large, oiled polythene bag, lightly tied, or a large saucepan with lid.

RISING: Stand the dough to rise until it doubles in size (about 30 minutes), and springs back when lightly pressed with a floured finger. Warmth will hasten the rising process—but it is not essential. In fact, average room temperature rising can give the best results because it controls the yeast and strengthens the dough, giving a loaf that rises better, bakes better and doesn't stale so quickly.

KNOCKING BACK: Turn the dough on to board again, divide into four and flatten each piece firmly with the knuckles to knock out the air bubbles, knead to make a firm dough (when kneading and moulding dough, it is important not to use too much flour for dusting as this might spoil the colour and texture of the loaf).

SHAPING: To make a tin loaf, shape each piece either by folding in three, or rolling up like a Swiss roll and tucking the ends under. The finally moulded dough piece should exactly fit the tin.

PROVING: Place each dough piece in a greased 1-lb. loaf tin, brush the top with salted water, put inside an oiled polythene bag, and put aside until the dough rises to the tops of the tins. Remove the polythene cover and brush with salted water again.

BAKING: Bake the loaves in the centre of a hot oven 450°F., Gas 8 for 30–40 minutes or until the loaves shrink slightly from the sides of the tin and the crust is deep golden brown. Take out of tin and cool on a rack. For a crustier loaf, turn the loaves out on to a baking sheet and bake for a further 5–10 minutes.

Quick Wheatmeal Bread

THIS QUANTITY MAKES UP 2 SMALL LOAVES OR 12 ROLLS

1 lb. mixed plain flours, wholemeal and white, in any proportion you like; 1 oz. fresh yeast or ½ oz. dried yeast (1 level tablespoon); 2 teaspoons each of sugar and salt; ½ pint water

Preparation: 25 minutes *Cooking time: about 30 minutes*

USING FRESH YEAST: Rub yeast into flour, salt and sugar, add all the water and mix to a soft dough, like scones, using one hand or a wooden spoon. Work to a smooth dough, adding more flour if needed, until the dough leaves the sides of the basin clean.

USING DRIED YEAST: Add a teaspoonful of sugar to a cupful of the water used in the recipe. (To get the best result this water should be warmed to 110°F. or hand-hot.) Sprinkle the dried yeast on top. Leave till frothy (10 minutes). Add to the flour, salt and remaining sugar with rest of liquid and mix and knead thoroughly on a floured board. The dough is now ready for use.

TO MAKE LOAVES: Half fill 2 well greased 1-lb. loaf tins or 4–5 in. flower-pots with dough. Put inside a large, greased polythene bag, loosely tied, and allow to rise to double size. Remove bag. Bake on middle shelf of hot oven, 450°F., Gas 8, for 30 to 40 minutes.
Note: It is a good idea to grease the flower-pot well before using and bake it empty in a hot oven first. This prevents the loaf sticking.

TO MAKE ROLLS: Flatten the dough to ½ in. thickness on a floured board. Cut into rounds with a 2½-in. cutter and dredge with flour, or divide dough into 12 pieces and roll into rounds in crushed cornflakes or cracked wheat. Place on a floured baking sheet, cover with greased polythene. Rise to double size and bake at top of the oven, 450°F., Gas 8, for 20 to 30 minutes. Surplus dough can be kept in a refrigerator in a loosely tied polythene bag or plastic container with lid for use next day.

To get a crusty finish, brush tops with salt and water and sprinkle with cornflakes or cracked wheat and bake 5 minutes longer. For a crisp light crust, brush with salad oil. For soft finish put rolls close together on the baking tin, brush with milk and dredge with flour.

Apricot and Walnut Bread

12 oz. risen wheatmeal dough (half the previous recipe); 4 oz. chopped dried apricots; 2 oz. broken walnuts; 1 oz. caster sugar; 1 oz. margarine

Preparation: 35 minutes *Cooking time: 30–40 minutes*

Good served well-buttered with a salad and cheese.

Work ingredients well together in a basin using one hand. Turn on to lightly floured board and shape to size of 1-lb. loaf tin. Put the dough in a well greased loaf tin inside a large greased polythene bag and leave to rise to within ½ in. of the top of the tin. Remove bag.

Bake in a 450°F., Gas 8 oven for 30 to 40 minutes. Remove from the oven, brush the loaf with a wet brush dipped in honey or syrup and cool on a wire tray.

Danish Pastries

For the yeast liquid: 1 level teaspoon caster sugar; 5 tablespoons lukewarm water; 2 level teaspoons dried yeast; 8 oz. plain flour (preferably a soft household flour); pinch salt; 1 oz. lard; 1 egg, beaten; 1 level tablespoon caster sugar; 5 oz. butter
For the almond paste: 3 oz. ground almonds; 3 oz. caster sugar; few drops almond essence; egg white
For the glaze: 1 egg, beaten with 1 tablespoon cold water
To finish: 4 oz. icing sugar, sifted; flaked almonds, lightly toasted; glacé cherries

Preparation: 40 minutes *Cooking time: about 15 minutes*

Get out several lightly greased baking trays.

Danish pastries, delicious, crisp, pastry layered confections are rewarding to bake at home. It's no good pretending that they are as easy as scones to make, because they are not. It takes time, about 2 hours from weighing up the ingredients to gorging the finished product, but of course other jobs can be done in between rolling and other processes. Follow these logical instructions and you will be surprised what fun they are to do. I have used dried yeast because it is easy to get. Should there be some of the pastries over for the next day serve them warmed up—they are best this way.

1. Prepare the yeast liquid. Mix the sugar with the water, stir until dissolved then sprinkle the yeast on top and leave it to stand until it is frothy, about 10 minutes. Sift the flour and salt into a bowl, add the lard cut in small pieces and rub it in with the fingertips until the mixture resembles fine breadcrumbs. Add the sugar, egg and yeast liquid all at once and mix it to a soft dough with a fork. When most of the flour has been worked in continue to work the mixture with the hands. If some of the dough sticks to the sides of the bowl add an extra tablespoon of flour to the dough.

Turn the dough on to a lightly floured board and knead it lightly for about 5 minutes or until it is smooth. Place the dough inside a lightly oiled polythene bag and leave it to rest in the refrigerator or other cool place for 10 minutes. Beat the butter in a bowl until it is soft.

2. Roll out the dough to form a 10-in. square. Spread the butter in a rectangle about 4½ in. wide in the centre of the dough but do not spread it to the top and bottom edges (leave a ½-in. margin) or the butter will ooze out when the dough is handled. Fold the two side edges into the centre so that they just overlap in the middle. Seal the bottom and top edges by pressing them with a rolling pin.

3. Roll out the dough to an oblong strip about three times as long as it is wide (about 5 inches by 15 inches). Fold the bottom third towards the middle and then bring the top third over to cover it. Make a mark with the knuckle in the dough to remind you that it has had one rolling. Put the dough into the polythene bag and leave it to rest in the refrigerator for 10 minutes. Remove the dough from the bag and turn it so that the open edge is on your left. Roll and fold the dough in the same manner as before. Make two marks on the dough with the knuckles. Return the dough to the bag and chill it again. Repeat the rolling, folding and chilling process a third time then roll out the pastry and use it as required.

While the pastry is being chilled for the third time prepare the almond paste by mixing the ground almonds, sugar and almond essence with just enough egg white to bind it together.

TO SHAPE THE PASTRIES:

(a) Crescents: (i) Roll out half the dough to form a 9-in. circle. Divide the circle into 8 sections. (ii) Cut a small lengthwise slit about one inch long near the pointed end. Place a small amount of almond paste at the wide base of each wedge. (iii) Roll up from the base towards the point and bend into a crescent shape.

(b) Windmill: (i) Roll out ¼ of the dough to form a 6-in. square. (ii) Cut the dough into 4 equal sized pieces. Place a small amount of almond paste in the centre of one square. Make cuts from each corner almost to the centre. (iii) Then lift the bottom left-hand corner of one triangle into the centre to cover part of the almond paste. Repeat with the remaining 3 sides to form a star. Repeat with the remaining squares.

When the pastries have been shaped put them on to the baking trays, allowing enough room for them to spread. Brush the pastries with egg glaze, cover them with a polythene bag and leave them at room temperature to prove until they look puffy, about 15 to 20 minutes. The proving temperature should be cooler than the temperature for proving bread or the butter will melt out of the pastries. When the pastries have proved, brush them again with egg glaze and bake them at 425°F., Gas 7, for about 12 to 15 minutes or until they are golden brown, then remove them from the oven and place them on a wire rack. Blend the icing sugar with sufficient water to make a rather runny glacé icing and spoon this over the pastries while they are still warm. Sprinkle some of them with lightly toasted flaked almonds or decorate with small pieces of glacé cherry.

Honey and Fruit Teabread

3 oz. butter; 8 oz. self-raising flour; 2 oz. caster sugar; 2 oz. currants; 2 oz. sultanas; 3 tablespoons clear honey; ¼ pint milk

Preparation: 15 minutes *Cooking time: about 1½ hours*

Get out a loaf cake tin approximately 4½ × 8 in. across the top. Set oven at 325°F., Gas 3.

Rub butter into sifted flour until mixture resembles fine breadcrumbs. Add sugar and fruit. Mix honey into milk, then blend with flour mixture to a slack dropping consistency. Turn into a greased and floured loaf tin, level top. Bake in oven at 325°F., Gas 3 for 1½ hours until well risen and golden. Cool, cut into slices and serve with butter.

Moist Gingerbread

1 lb. plain flour; pinch salt; 2 level teaspoons ground ginger; 4 oz. granulated sugar; 8 oz. stoned raisins, roughly chopped; 4 oz. margarine; 8 oz. treacle; 1 level teaspoon bicarbonate of soda; ¼ pint milk; 1 egg, beaten; 12 sugar cubes, crushed

Preparation: 15 minutes *Cooking time: about 1½ hours*

Get out a 12 × 8 × 2 in. tin, a small meat tin will do, grease and line with greased greaseproof paper.

Set oven at 325°F., Gas 3.

Sift the flour, salt and ginger into a bowl. Add the sugar and raisins. Melt the fat with the treacle in a pan, dissolve the bicarbonate of soda in a little of the milk and add to the fat and treacle. Make a well in the centre of the dry ingredients and add the melted mixture with the egg. Stir well and add enough of the milk to make a fairly soft mixture. Put into the prepared tin, sprinkle with the crushed sugar lumps and bake for 1½ hours or until a skewer inserted in the centre of the gingerbread comes out clean. Turn out to cool on a wire rack. Eat either the day it is made or store in a tin for at least five days to mature.

Brown Scones

MAKES 14 HALVES

8 oz. brown self-raising flour; pinch of salt; 2 oz. butter; 1 oz. caster sugar; approx. ¼ pint milk; butter; black cherry jam; whipped cream

Preparation: 10 minutes *Cooking time: about 15 minutes*

Set oven at 425°F., Gas 7.

Get out a baking sheet.

Sift flour and salt into a mixing bowl. Rub in butter finely with fingertips and then stir in sugar. Bind with sufficient milk to make a soft but not sticky dough. Turn out on to a board sprinkled with a little of the brown flour and roll out to ½ in. thickness. Cut into 2½-in. rounds and place on a lightly greased baking sheet. Bake towards top of the oven (425°F., Gas 7) for 15–20 minutes or until well risen and cooked through. Place on a wire rack to cool. Whilst still slightly warm split and spread each half with butter and a little black cherry jam. Serve with whipped cream.

CAKES

Chocolate and Almond Cake

3 oz. self-raising flour; 1½ oz. cocoa; 6 oz. butter; 6 oz. caster sugar; 4 eggs, beaten; 3 oz. ground almonds; 1 oz. blanched, split almonds

Preparation: 15 minutes *Cooking time: 1½ hours*

Get out a 7-in. diameter cake tin, grease and line with greased greaseproof paper.

Set oven at 325°F., Gas 3.

This cake keeps well and, if liked, may be iced with lemon glacé icing.

Sift the flour and cocoa into a bowl and set it on one side. Beat the butter until it is soft then add the sugar and continue to beat until the mixture is light and fluffy. Add the beaten egg a teaspoon at a time, beating well after each addition so that the mixture does not curdle. Fold in the sifted flour and cocoa and finally the ground almonds. Turn the mixture into the prepared tin, arrange the blanched almonds on top and bake the cake for 1½ hours or until the top of the cake springs back into shape when lightly pressed. Turn the cake out to cool on a wire rack.

Sticky Ginger Cake

8 oz. plain flour; 2 level teaspoons ground ginger; 4 oz. margarine; 4 oz. soft brown sugar; 2 eggs, beaten; 6 level tablespoons treacle; 2 oz. seedless raisins; 2 oz. sultanas; ⅛ pint (6 tablespoons) milk; 1 level teaspoon bicarbonate of soda

Preparation: 15 minutes *Baking time: about 1¼ hours*

Get out a 7-in. square cake tin, grease and line.

Set oven at 325°F., Gas 3.

If you like a tacky ginger cake make this one. Don't be worried that it is not dark when it comes out of the oven. After a few days' maturing it will begin to darken. It is ready to eat after a week and will keep for at least three.

Sift together the flour and ginger. Cream the margarine until it is soft, add the sugar and continue to beat until the mixture is light and fluffy. Add the egg a little at a time, beating well and keeping the mixture stiff. Fold the sifted flour into the mixture alternately with the treacle. Mix thoroughly and stir in the raisins and sultanas. Warm the milk in a small pan to blood heat then add the bicarbonate of soda. Stir the milk into the gingerbread mixture and mix to a smooth batter. Pour this thick batter into the prepared tin and bake it for 1¼ hours, or until a skewer inserted in the centre of the cake comes out clean. Turn it out to cool on a wire rack and when it is cold store it in an airtight tin.

Treacle Cake

4 oz. butter; 3 oz. caster sugar; 2 eggs; 5 level tablespoons (6 oz.) black treacle; 4 oz. self-raising flour; 1 teaspoon mixed spice; 4 oz. sultanas; sifted icing sugar for topping

Preparation: 15 minutes *Cooking time: 1¼–1½ hours*

Get out 7-in. diameter tin.

Set oven at 300°F., Gas 2.

This is the best weekend cake that I know because it is so spicy and moist. Line a 7-in. diameter tin with greased greaseproof paper. Cream butter and sugar together until light and fluffy. Whisk eggs and beat well into creamed mixture. Add black treacle and sift in flour and mixed spice. Fold in with a metal spoon, stir in sultanas and turn into prepared tin. Bake on shelf above centre of the oven (300°F., Gas 2) for 1¼–1½ hours or until well risen and cooked through. Turn out on to wire rack. Just before serving place a cooling rack over the cake and shake icing sugar through this to give a decorative effect.

Glazed Nut and Cherry Cake—Baked in a Loaf Tin

8 oz. self-raising flour; 6 oz. butter; 6 oz. caster sugar; 3 eggs, beaten; 6 tablespoons milk; 2½ oz. glacé cherries, quartered; 1 oz. hazel or walnuts, coarsely chopped
For the topping: 1½ oz. icing sugar, sieved; water; 1 oz. hazel or walnuts, halved; 1½ oz. glacé cherries, halved

Preparation: 20 minutes *Cooking time: about 1 hour*

Get out a 2-lb. (3-pint capacity) loaf tin, grease and line.
Sift the flour. Cream together the butter and sugar until light and fluffy. Beat in the egg a little at a time, beating well after each addition. Add a tablespoon of the flour with the last amount of egg. Fold the rest of the flour into the mixture then add the milk, cherries and nuts. Turn the mixture into the prepared loaf tin and bake it at 350°F., Gas 4, for 55–60 minutes until pale golden and the top of the loaf springs back into shape when lightly pressed. Turn the loaf out to cool on a wire rack.

FOR THE TOPPING: Mix the sieved icing sugar in a bowl with enough warm water to make a thin glacé icing. Spread a thin layer of icing on top of the cake, roughly arrange the cherries and nuts over this, then spoon the remainder of the icing on top of the fruit and nuts. Let some of the icing run down the sides of the loaf. Leave the icing to set before putting the cake in a tin.

Almond and Honey Cake

4 oz. butter; 4 oz. caster sugar; 2 eggs, beaten; 1 level tablespoon clear honey; 5 oz. self-raising flour; 1 oz. ground almonds; about 2 tablespoons milk
For the icing: 4 oz. butter; 2 level tablespoons clear honey; 2 teaspoons lemon juice; 12 oz. icing sugar, sifted; 4 oz. blanched, shredded, toasted almonds

Preparation: 20 minutes *Cooking time: about 20 minutes*

Get out two 7½-in. sandwich tins greased and the bases lined.
Set oven at 375°F., Gas 5.
This is a special cake—you really can taste the honey.

Cream the butter until it is soft then add the sugar and continue to cream the mixture until it is light and fluffy. Beat in the eggs a little at a time, beating well after each addition. Blend in the honey and then the flour and ground almonds. Add enough milk to give a soft dropping consistency. Divide the mixture between the two tins and bake it for about 15 to 20 minutes or until the centre of the cakes will spring back into place when lightly pressed with the finger. Leave the cakes to cool on a wire rack.

Meanwhile prepare the icing. Put the butter, honey and lemon juice into a small pan and heat gently until the butter has melted. Pour this warmed mixture on to the icing sugar, stir well and add just enough warm water to bind all the ingredients smoothly together. Sandwich the two cakes together with about one-third of the icing. Set aside about one heaped tablespoon of the remaining icing and add enough water to the rest to make it a thick coating consistency. Pour the coating icing over the top and sides of the cake, spreading it over the sides if necessary. Leave it for a few minutes to cool slightly then scatter the prepared almonds over the top. Put the remaining icing into a piping bag fitted with a star nozzle and pipe small whirls of cream round the top of the cake. Dust the cake lightly with sifted icing sugar and put one or two pieces of almond on top of each whirl of icing.

Tia Maria Coffee Cake

3 large eggs; 3 oz. caster sugar; 1 tablespoon hot water; 3 oz. plain flour

For the coffee butter cream filling: 12 oz. icing sugar, sifted; 2 tablespoons coffee essence; 2 tablespoons Tia Maria or rum; 6 oz. butter, softened; 2 oz. crystallized ginger, chopped

For decoration: 6 oz. icing sugar, sifted; 1 tablespoon coffee essence; 2 oz. nibbed almonds, lightly toasted; thin slices crystallized ginger

Preparation: 25 minutes *Cooking time: 25 minutes*

Get out two $7\frac{1}{2}$-in. straight-sided sandwich tins lined with greased greaseproof paper.

Set oven at 375°F., Gas 5.

Place the eggs and sugar in a bowl and place the bowl over a pan of hot water. Whisk until the mixture is very pale in colour and thick and mousse-like. Remove from the heat and with a metal spoon carefully fold in half the sifted flour. Add the water, then the remaining flour in the same way. Divide the mixture between the two tins and bake for 20–25 minutes or until the centre of each sponge springs back when pressed lightly. Turn out to cool on a wire rack.

PREPARE THE FILLING: Blend together the coffee essence and Tia Maria. Cream the butter until soft then add the icing sugar a little at a time, beating well after each addition. Cut each cake in half and sandwich together again with some of the filling. Mix the chopped ginger with some of the filling and use to sandwich the two cakes together. Thinly coat the sides of the cake with filling.

FOR THE ICING: Blend together the remaining icing sugar and coffee. Add a little water if necessary to give a stiff coating consistency. Pour over the top of the cake and leave to set.

Press the almonds against the sides of the cake with a palette knife. Using a piping bag fitted with a large star pipe decorate the edge of the cake with rosettes using the remaining filling. Place a slice of crystallized ginger on top of each rosette.

Swiss Roll

2 large eggs; 2 oz. caster sugar; 2 oz. self-raising flour; 1 tablespoon hot water; 3 tablespoons strawberry jam, warmed

Preparation: 15 minutes *Cooking time: about 10 minutes*

Get out two 7½-in. straight-sided sandwich tins lined with greased greaseproof paper.

Set oven at 400°F., Gas 6.

Place the eggs and sugar in a bowl and whisk with a rotary whisk until the mixture is light and creamy and the whisk leaves a trail when lifted out of the mixture. If using an electric mixer take care not to let the mixture get too stiff as it will then be difficult to fold the flour in evenly. Fold in half the sifted flour, using a metal spoon, then fold in the water, then the remainder of the flour. Turn the mixture into the prepared tin and bake for about 10 minutes or until the sponge springs back when pressed gently.

Turn out on to greaseproof paper dredged with caster sugar. As quickly as possible trim the edges of the sponge. Spread with the jam. Roll up from the narrow side, tuck the flap underneath. Dredge with caster sugar and leave to cool.

Simnel Cake

FOR THE GRAND OCCASION

6 oz. butter; 6 oz. soft brown sugar; finely grated rind of 2 lemons; 4 eggs; 6 oz. plain flour; 2 rounded teaspoons mixed spice; 4 oz. sultanas; 6 oz. seedless raisins; 4 oz. chopped mixed peel; 4 oz. chopped glacé cherries; 2–3 tablespoons warmed sieved apricot jam; Easter chick for decoration
Almond paste: 10 oz. ground almonds; 5 oz. caster sugar; 5 oz. icing sugar; 1 egg; 1 tablespoon lemon juice; ½ teaspoon almond essence

Preparation: 30 minutes *Cooking time: 2½–3 hours*

Get out an 8-in. diameter tin.

This rich fruit cake, baked with a layer of almond paste in the middle, used to be given by daughters to their mothers on Mothering Sunday, though it was often not cut until Easter Day. Nowadays it is more often made as an Easter Cake and is decorated with chickens, eggs or flowers, and has almond paste on top also.

Line an 8-in. cake tin with greased greaseproof paper. Cream butter together with soft brown sugar and lemon rind until light and fluffy. Lightly whisk eggs together and beat half into the creamed mixture with a little of the sifted flour. Beat well, gradually adding the remainder of the eggs. Add mixed spice to the rest of the flour and sift into the creamed mixture. Fold in carefully with a metal spoon. Stir in sultanas, raisins, chopped mixed peel and cherries. Turn half the mixture into the prepared tin and smooth top with a knife. Roll out one-third of the prepared almond paste into an 8-in. round and place on top of the mixture in the tin. Cover with remaining cake mixture and once again smooth top with a knife. Bake at 300°F., Gas 2 for 2½–3 hours or until cooked through when tested with skewer. Leave to cool in tin for 10 minutes before turning out on to a wire cooling rack. Strip off lining papers. When cold and ready for decoration brush the top of the cake with warmed, sieved apricot jam. Roll out half the remaining almond paste into a round to cover top of the cake, using a rolling-pin to give a smooth flat surface. Brush round top outer edge with remaining apricot jam. Reserve a little of the remaining almond paste and roll the rest into 11 balls for top of cake. Roll out remainder into a long sausage shape and place round the outer edge of the cake on top of the apricot jam. Seal well, pressing top and round sides of roll with prongs of fork to give a decorative effect then arrange and fix the 11 balls on top of this in a circle. If a brown topping is preferred on the cake it may be placed under a grill on a gentle heat until just golden in colour. Place an Easter chick in position on top of the cake. Store in an airtight tin till required.

TO MAKE UP THE ALMOND PASTE: Place ground almonds in mixing bowl with caster sugar and sifted icing sugar. Make a well in the centre of the dry ingredients and add lightly whisked egg, strained lemon juice and flavourings. Bind to fairly stiff dough, knead lightly till smooth on sugared board.

Family Fruit Cake

Make the Simnel Cake without the almond paste. Bake in an 8-in. tin for about 2¼–2½ hours at 300°F., Gas 2, until cooked through and when speared with a fine skewer it comes out clean.

Rum Dessert Cake

FOR THE GRAND OCCASION

4 oz. caster sugar; 3 oz. self-raising flour; 1 oz. cocoa; 4 eggs; 3 tablespoons salad oil
Filling: 5 oz. butter; 8 oz. sieved icing sugar; 3 tablespoons rum
Icing: about 4 tablespoons evaporated milk; 2 tablespoons rum; 6 oz. plain chocolate
Decoration: Grated chocolate

Preparation: 25 minutes *Cooking time: about 45 minutes*

Set oven at 350°F., Gas 4.

Get out an 8-in. round cake tin and line with greased greaseproof paper.

Sieve the flour and cocoa. Whisk the eggs with sugar until the mixture is light and creamy and the whisk leaves a trail when lifted out of the mixture. Fold in sieved flour and cocoa, lastly fold in oil gently. Turn into prepared tin and bake at 350°F., Gas 4 for about 45 minutes. Turn out and leave to cool on a wire rack. Split into 4 rounds and spread the bottom three with butter cream flavoured to taste with about 3 tablespoons of rum. Do not allow butter to become oily before creaming as the rum would then cause the mixture to curdle.

TO MAKE ICING: Heat evaporated milk and rum in a pan over low heat until very hot but not boiling. Remove from heat and add broken-up chocolate. Stir until the chocolate has dissolved, returning to a gentle heat if necessary. Cool, stirring, until the icing just coats the wooden spoon. If you cool it too much don't worry, just warm it up again. Pour the icing over the cake and leave to set. When nearly set scatter with grated chocolate.

This cake keeps particularly well.

Chocolate and Orange Ring Cake

8 oz. self-raising flour; 2 oz. cocoa; 8 oz. butter; 6 oz. soft brown sugar; finely grated rind of 1 orange; 4 oz. black treacle; 4 eggs, blended

For the orange glacé icing: 8 oz. icing sugar, sifted; juice of 1 orange; 2 teaspoons salad oil; little water; little orange colouring

Preparation: 25 minutes *Cooking time: about 1 hour*

Set oven at 350°F., Gas 4.

Get out a 3½-pint capacity ring mould.

Grease the ring mould very thoroughly and put a strip of greased greaseproof paper into the base of the mould to make sure the cake comes out well. Sift the flour and cocoa. Cream the butter until it is soft, then add the sugar and orange rind and continue to beat until the mixture is light and fluffy. Beat in the egg a little at a time, beating well after each addition, add some of the flour with the last amount of egg. Finally blend in the rest of the sifted flour and cocoa and treacle and mix until it is smooth. Put the mixture into the prepared tin and bake it for about 1 hour or until it is well risen and will spring back into place when lightly pressed with the finger. Remove the cake from the oven and leave it to cool for a few minutes before turning it out, very carefully, on to a wire rack.

When the cake is cold blend the orange juice and salad oil with the icing sugar, adding just enough water to make a fairly stiff glacé icing. A few drops of colouring may be added, if liked. Spoon the icing over the top of the cake, allowing it to fall in trickles down the sides.

Sugar-Topped Currant Cakes

MAKES ABOUT 18

8 oz. self-raising flour; pinch of salt; 6 oz. butter; 6 oz. caster sugar; grated rind of 1 lemon; 6 oz. currants and sultanas mixed; 1 oz. candied peel, finely chopped; 2 eggs; milk to mix; 8 sugar cubes, roughly crushed

Preparation: 15 minutes *Cooking time: about 15 minutes*

Set oven at 400°F., Gas 6.

Get out two 9-holed patty tins well greased.

These small buns are the kind to pop in the oven after the Sunday joint when you hear unexpectedly there are to be hoards for tea. Best eaten the day that they are made.

Sift the flour and salt into a bowl. Cut the fat into small pieces then rub it into the flour until the mixture resembles fine breadcrumbs. Add the sugar, lemon rind, dried fruit and peel. Make a well in the centre of the ingredients and add the eggs with enough milk to mix to a fairly stiff consistency. Spoon into patty tins. Top with the crushed sugar. Bake for 15 minutes or until pale golden brown. Cool on a wire rack.

Glazed Raspberry Tarts

MAKES 9

Tartlet cases: 4 oz. plain flour; $\frac{1}{4}$ teaspoon salt; $2\frac{1}{2}$ oz. butter; $\frac{1}{2}$ oz. caster sugar; about 4 teaspoons water

Filling: $\frac{1}{2}$ lb. fresh raspberries; 3 level tablespoons red currant jelly; 1 tablespoon water

Preparation: 20 minutes *Cooking time: about 15 minutes*

Set oven at 375°F., Gas 5.

Get out a 9-holed patty tin.

The same tarts may also be filled with other fruits in season.

Make shortcrust pastry in the usual way. Roll out and cut out nine 2-in. circles, line patty tins with these pressing down well, prick base and chill. Bake for about 15 minutes until pale golden brown, cool on a wire rack.

When the tartlet cases are cold, arrange raspberries in the centre. Sieve the red currant jelly into a small pan and add the water; heat slowly, stirring occasionally, until smooth. Spoon over the glaze.

Orange Victoria Sandwich

4 oz. butter; 1 orange; 4 oz. caster sugar; 2 eggs, beaten; 4 oz. self-raising flour; little milk
For the butter icing: 1½ oz. butter; 3 oz. icing sugar, sifted
For the glacé icing: 4 oz. icing sugar, sifted; dash of orange colouring

Preparation: 25 minutes *Cooking time: about 20 minutes*

Get out two 7-in. straight-sided sandwich tins well greased and the bases lined with a disc of greased greaseproof paper.

Set the oven at 350°F., Gas 4.

Beat the butter in a bowl until it is soft then add the finely-grated rind of half the orange with the caster sugar and continue to beat the mixture until it is light and fluffy. Add the egg a teaspoon at a time, beating well after each addition, and add a little of the flour with the last amount of egg. Fold in the rest of the flour, adding a little milk if necessary to make a soft dropping consistency—so that it drops off the spoon fairly easily. Divide the mixture between the tins and bake the sponges at 350°F., Gas 4 for 20 minutes, or until the centre of the sponges will spring back into place when lightly pressed with the finger. Turn the sponges out to cool on a wire rack.

While the sponges are cooking prepare the butter cream. Beat the butter in a small bowl until it is soft, then add the icing sugar and the strained juice of half the orange and continue to beat the mixture until it is light and fluffy. When the sponges are cold, sandwich them together with the butter cream.

Prepare the glacé icing. Peel the zest from the remaining half orange with a potato peeler and cut it into very thin strips. Put these into a small pan, cover them with water and bring to boiling point then simmer them for 5 minutes or until they are tender. Drain them thoroughly and then dry them on absorbent kitchen paper. Add the juice from the remaining half orange to the icing sugar with the orange strips and just enough water to make a stiff glacé icing. A few drops of orange colouring may also be added if liked. Pour the icing over the top of the cake and leave it to set before serving.

Florentines

MAKES ABOUT 15

2 oz. butter; 2 oz. caster sugar; 2 oz. chopped nuts; ½ oz. sultanas; ½ oz. candied peel; ½ oz. glacé cherries, chopped; 1 tablespoon double cream; 2 oz. melted plain chocolate

Preparation: 20 minutes *Cooking time: about 10 minutes*

Get out two baking trays.

Set the oven at 350°F., Gas 4.

Grease and flour the baking trays. Melt the butter in a pan, add the sugar and boil it for one minute only. Blend in all the other ingredients except the chocolate. Place small portions of the mixture on the prepared baking trays, leaving plenty of space between each as the mixture spreads. Bake at 350°F., Gas 4, for about 10 minutes or until the Florentines are golden brown. Remove them from the oven, neaten the edges and flatten them with a palette knife. Leave them to cool slightly before removing them from the baking tray and putting them on greaseproof paper. When they are cold brush the flat side of each Florentine with melted chocolate and make a zig-zag impression with a fork over the chocolate before it sets.

Meringues

MAKES 8 PAIRS

2 egg whites; 4 oz. caster sugar

Preparation: 15 minutes *Cooking time: about 2 hours*

Get out 2 large baking sheets.

Set the oven at 225°F., Gas $\frac{1}{4}$.

Oil the baking sheets well or line them with non-stick household vegetable parchment.

Put the egg whites into a china or ovenglass mixing bowl. Whisk them with a rotary whisk until they are very stiff. Continue to whisk, adding the sugar a level teaspoonful at a time and whisking well after each addition, until all the sugar has been included. Using two wet dessertspoons, spoon the meringue on to the prepared sheets, or pipe it in rosette shapes on to the sheets. Sprinkle with caster sugar and dry them off in the oven (225°F., Gas $\frac{1}{4}$) for $1\frac{1}{2}$ to 2 hours. Remove the meringues from the oven and, when they are cold, sandwich them together with whipped cream.

BISCUITS

Butter Shortbread

4 oz. plain flour; 2 oz. cornflour; 4 oz. butter; 2 oz. caster sugar; finely grated rind of 1 orange or lemon; extra caster sugar

Preparation: 15 minutes *Cooking time: about 35 minutes*

Set oven at 325°F., Gas 3.

Get out 2 large baking trays.

I am told that this recipe once won fame in a Scottish W.I. baking competition—no wonder it is so good.

Sift together the flour and cornflour. Cream the butter until it is soft then add the 2 oz. caster sugar and lemon or orange rind and continue to beat until the mixture is light and fluffy. Then work in the flour a tablespoon at a time. Knead together and divide in two. Shape into two rounds. Lift one of the shortbread rounds on to the baking sheet (a large one is needed as the shortbread will spread a little when it is baking). Flatten the dough with the knuckles to form a 7-in. circle. Do the same with the other round. Pinch the edges and prick it well with a fork. Mark them each into 8 sections with the back of a knife then sprinkle with the extra caster sugar. Leave the shortbread to chill in the refrigerator for 15 minutes then bake it for 35 minutes or until it is pale golden brown. Leave it to cool on the baking tray for a few minutes then lift it on to a wire rack to finish cooling.

Macaroons

MAKES 16

2 large egg whites; 4 oz. ground almonds; 6 oz. caster sugar; 1 oz. ground rice; few drops almond essence; 8 blanched almonds

Preparation: 15 minutes *Cooking time: about 30 minutes*

Set oven at 300°F., Gas 2.

Get out two large baking trays lined preferably with rice paper or else non-stick household parchment or greased greaseproof paper.

Firstly put a little egg white (about 1 teaspoon) into a small bowl for brushing over the macaroons before baking. Then whisk the remaining egg white until it forms soft peaks. Fold in the ground almonds, sugar, ground rice and almond essence. Mix well. Put heaped teaspoonfuls of the mixture on to the rice paper and smooth them out with the back of the spoon to form circles (do not flatten them too much). Put half a blanched almond in the centre of each macaroon and brush the tops of the macaroons with egg white. Bake for about 25 to 30 minutes or until the macaroons are pale golden. Allow them to cool slightly before removing them from the baking tray. Remove any excess rice paper round the edge of the macaroons. If using non-stick household parchment peel it away from the macaroons.

Flapjacks

MAKES 10 PIECES

4 oz. butter; 1 oz. caster sugar; 8 oz. rolled oats; $\frac{1}{4}$ level teaspoon salt; 4 oz. (2 rounded tablespoons) golden syrup, warmed

Preparation: 15 minutes *Cooking time: about 30 minutes*

Set oven at 350°F., Gas 4.

Get out a 7-in. square shallow tin, greased.

Cream the butter in a bowl until it is soft. Add the sugar and cream until light and fluffy. Stir in the oats, salt and syrup. Mix thoroughly then turn into the prepared tin.

Bake at 350°F., Gas 4, for about 30 minutes or until the mixture is golden brown and just firm to the touch. Remove from the oven, leave to cool for a few minutes then cut into 10 fingers. Leave to cool completely before removing from the tin.

Viennese Shortbread Biscuits

MAKES ABOUT 10 PAIRS

4 oz. butter; 1 oz. icing sugar, sifted; 5 oz. plain flour; few drops milk if necessary

Butter cream filling: 2 oz. butter; 4 oz. icing sugar, sifted; 1 oz. cooking chocolate, melted

Preparation: 20 minutes *Cooking time: about 15 minutes*

Set oven at 375°F., Gas 5.

Get out a large baking sheet, greased.

These are shortbread fingers sandwiched together with chocolate butter cream.

Cream the butter with the icing sugar until really soft. Stir in the sifted flour and mix well. If the mixture seems rather stiff a little milk may be added. Put the mixture into a piping bag fitted with a large star pipe. Pipe the mixture on to the baking sheet in small circles, shells, or fingers, making sure that there are an even number of each shape. Leave in the refrigerator or other cold place for at least 15 minutes to chill. Bake for about 10–15 minutes or until the biscuits are just beginning to turn golden brown. Cool on a wire rack.

Cream together the butter and icing sugar for the filling. Add the chocolate and mix well. When the biscuits are cold, sandwich in pairs with the butter cream. Dust the tops with a little sifted icing sugar.

Boter Moppen

MAKES ABOUT 32

8 oz. plain flour; pinch of salt; 6 oz. butter; finely grated rind of ½ a lemon; 4 oz. caster sugar; 1 oz. granulated sugar

Preparation: 15 minutes *Cooking time: about 25 minutes*

Set oven at 325°F., Gas 3.

Get out 2 baking trays, greased.

No cutters needed for this—make a long sausage shape of shortbread. Chill, then cut off rounds and bake.

Sift the flour and salt into a bowl. Cream the butter until soft, add the lemon rind and caster sugar and beat until light and fluffy. Blend in the flour and mix until smooth. Divide the mixture into two equal portions. Roll both out to form two 6-in. long sausage shapes. Roll in the granulated sugar. Wrap in foil then chill in the refrigerator until firm. Cut each sausage into about 16 slices and place the slices on the baking trays. Allow room for them to spread. Bake for about 25 minutes or until the biscuits are pale golden at the edges.

Anzac Biscuits

MAKES 30

2 oz. golden syrup (1 heaped tablespoon); 5 oz. butter; 4 oz. caster sugar; 3 oz. rolled oats; 2 oz. desiccated coconut; 5 oz. plain flour; 2 level teaspoons bicarbonate of soda; 1 tablespoon hot water

Preparation: 15 minutes *Cooking time: about 20 minutes*

Set oven at 325°F., Gas 3.

Get out 2 baking trays, greased.

Put the syrup, butter and caster sugar into a pan, melt over a low heat. Remove the pan from the heat and stir in the dry ingredients. Place the bicarbonate of soda in a small bowl and dissolve with the hot water. Add to the other ingredients. Leave to cool for a few minutes. Roll into about 30 balls and place on the baking trays, leaving plenty of room between each for spreading. Bake for about 20 minutes or until the biscuits have browned evenly. Remove from the oven and leave on the baking trays for a few moments to harden. Cool on a wire rack.

Almond Crisps

MAKES ABOUT 60

6 oz. plain flour; 3 eggs; $1\frac{1}{2}$ teaspoons water; 9 oz. caster sugar; $\frac{1}{4}$ teaspoon almond essence; sugar for dredging

Preparation: 15 minutes *Cooking time: about 15 minutes*

Set oven at 325°F., Gas 3.

These are the kind of biscuits that go well with ice-cream and mousses—the recipe makes masses but they keep well in a tin.

Line some baking trays with oiled greaseproof paper or non-stick household parchment. Sieve the flour. Break the eggs into a bowl, add the water and whisk well together. Gradually add the sugar, whisking after each addition. Continue to whisk until the mixture is thick and pale in colour. Fold in the sifted flour, using a metal spoon. Add the essence at the same time. Place teaspoonfuls of the mixture on the prepared baking trays and bake at 325°F., Gas 3, for 15 to 20 minutes, or until pale golden brown. Allow to cool and dredge with sugar.

Easter Biscuits

MAKES 24

8 oz. butter; 6 oz. caster sugar; finely-grated rind 1 lemon; pinch salt; 3 egg yolks; 12 oz. plain flour; 2 oz. currants; 2 oz. mixed peel; 1 egg white; a little caster sugar

Preparation: 15 minutes *Cooking time: about 20 minutes*

Set oven at 350°F., Gas 4.

Cream butter with caster sugar, grated lemon rind and salt until light and fluffy. Beat in the separated egg yolks and then sift in the flour. Stir in currants and mixed peel, then knead to a smooth dough. Place in refrigerator or cool place for about 1 hour until the dough becomes firm. Roll out on a lightly floured board to just under $\frac{1}{4}$-in. thickness and cut into 3-in. rounds with a fluted cutter. Transfer to a lightly greased baking sheet. Brush tops with the lightly whisked egg white and sprinkle with caster sugar. Cook at 350°F., Gas 4 for 15–20 minutes or until pale golden and cooked through. Transfer to cooling rack and store in an airtight tin until required.

THINGS THAT MAY GO WRONG IN CAKE MAKING

It is very important in the first place to weigh the quantities accurately. Follow the recipe implicitly and use a tin of the right size for the amount of mixture.

Speckling on top of the cake

Too coarse sugar used, i.e. granulated or coarse brown sugar
Too much sugar
Not creaming butter and sugar for long enough

Badly cracked top or risen to a peak in the centre

Too much raising agent
The cake cooked on too high a shelf in the oven (unless otherwise stated cakes should be placed in the middle of the oven)
Too stiff mixture
Oven too hot
Cake tin not large enough for the amount of mixture

Top sunk in the middle

Too much raising agent
Too cool an oven—middle hasn't risen
Mixture too soft
Taking out of the oven before being cooked through, causing it to sink whilst cooling
Banging the oven door during baking, letting cold air in
In a gingerbread or ginger cake—too much treacle

Fruit dropped to the bottom

Glacé cherries dropping to the bottom? Cut them in half, wash off the excess syrup and dry. Tossing in flour helps
Fruit too large. Cut up before adding to cake mixture
Oven too slow
Mixture too slack and runny
Fruit wet when added to cake mixture

Uneven and holey texture

Uneven mixing
Beating in the flour instead of gently folding it in
In rubbed-in cakes, the fat and flour not rubbed in well enough
Too much baking powder

Dry and crumbly

Baking at too high a temperature
Baking for too long, usually too slowly
Too much baking powder

Hard crust on top

Too much sugar
Too large a tin for the amount of mixture
Over baking

Burnt fruit on top and outside of fruit cake

Too hot an oven
Not lining cake tin sufficiently or, to prevent further browning, not protecting the top with double thickness of greaseproof when it has baked a light brown colour

Rapid Staling

Mixture too dry

Not rich enough mixture—rich cakes keep better than plain cakes made with a large proportion of flour. Butter to my mind makes the cakes which keep best

Bad storage. Cool cakes completely then store in a cake tin not too big for the size of cake, or wrap in foil. If keeping for a length of time wrap in greaseproof paper then foil. Store in cool dry larder.

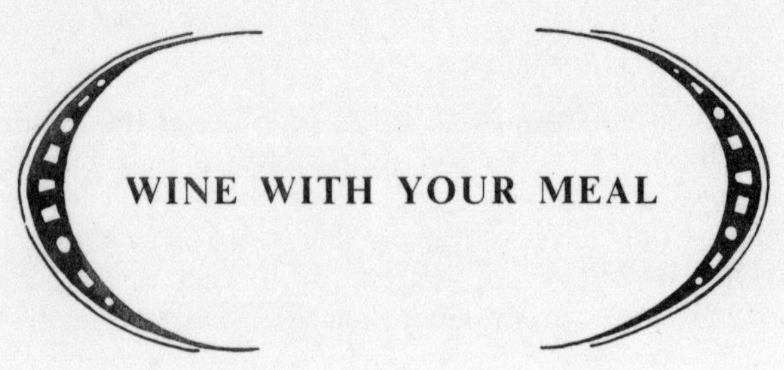

WINE WITH YOUR MEAL

by PAUL HUNNINGS

You are giving a dinner party and you want to serve wine. This chapter is intended for those who are aware that wine is complementary to good food but who do not have any deep knowledge of the subject.

In the same way that food preparation is considered the female prerogative, wine is considered to be the male prerogative, so my first advice is to delegate everything to do with wine to your husband or boy-friend. However, there are occasions when he may not have had time to buy the wine or has been delayed at the office. It is therefore advisable for you to know the fundamentals just in case.

What wine should I have with the meal?

This depends on the meal. As soon as you have decided the menu, you can choose the wine or wines to be drunk with the meal.

It is very difficult to draw a hard and fast line as to what wine should be served with any particular dish. The individual preferences of your guests are the most important factor. If you know that your guests always like to drink, say, white wine irrespective of the food which is being served, then have white wine; or you could of course serve both and please everyone!

However, experience indicates that certain wines go best with certain foods. Some suggestions, based on these findings, are given below:

As an aperitif	Dry sherry, dry Madeira or Champagne
Hors d'Oeuvre	Sherry or dry white wine

Oysters	White Burgundy, Graves, Champagne or Moselle
Soup	Dry sherry or dry Madeira
Fish	White Burgundy, Graves, Champagne, Hock, Moselle or Alsatian
Game and Meat	Claret, red Burgundy, red Rhône wines, or firm-bodied Hock
Puddings	Sauternes, Barsac, Champagne or a rich Hock
Cheese	Port, rich sherry, Burgundy or Hock
Dessert	Port, rich sherry or Madeira
Coffee	Brandy or liqueurs

Rosé wines, which in character can be said to be midway between red and white wines, can be drunk throughout informal meals. Champagne goes with all food and also can be drunk throughout a meal. With vinegary dressed salads and highly spiced foods it is best to avoid serving fine wines of either colour as the flavour of the food will smother the attributes of the wine.

What wine do I choose?

The first thing to do is to make a friend of your wine merchant. Tell him the kind of wine you want and ask him to recommend a particular vintage, shipper, etc. When a wine is produced in a particular year the year is written on the label. These wines are called 'vintage' wines. Where there is no mention of the year the wines are called 'non-vintage'. Some years are better than others and a vintage chart, produced by many wine merchants, is invaluable. This type of chart compares the vintages and gives them a number of marks for each year so that the vintage with the highest number of marks is generally considered to be the best. Here again there are exceptions but the chart is very useful as a guide.

At what temperature should I serve the wine?

Red wines should be served at room temperature. Take the bottle out of the wine cupboard in plenty of time, stand it in the dining-room and let it come to room temperature slowly of its own accord.

White wine, and also dry sherry and Champagne, should be served slightly chilled. If it is served too cold some of the flavour and bouquet will be lost. Cooling should be achieved by placing the wine in an ice-bucket or a refrigerator for a short period (a maximum of three hours before drinking).

For all wines any adjustment to the temperature of the wine should be made gradually; no wine should be chilled or heated suddenly. Under no circumstances should the bottle be immersed in hot water or placed in front of a fire. Sudden changes of temperature are most detrimental to any wine.

Opening the bottle, how and when?

Try not to move the bottle any more than is absolutely necessary. Vintage red wines often have a sediment at the bottom of the bottle, which should not be disturbed.

Before opening the wine, remove the metal capsule round the cork. Wipe the cork and top of the bottle with a damp cloth first and then with a brush kept specially for this purpose—an old toothbrush will do. This helps to remove any foreign particles from the crevice between the cork and the bottle lip. Withdraw the cork gently and then wipe the lip of the bottle carefully in order to remove any foreign particles which may remain.

I cannot over-emphasize the importance of allowing wines to 'breathe', particularly young red wines. If you open a non-vintage red wine as much as three hours before the meal and keep the cork out so that the wine can 'breathe', you will find that it is a much more pleasant wine to drink.

Non-vintage wines	open 3 hours before meal
Vintage wines, up to 4 years old	open $1\frac{1}{2}$ hours before meal
Vintage wines, 4–8 years old	open 1 hour before meal
Vintage wines, 8 years old and over	open $\frac{1}{4}$–$\frac{1}{2}$ hour before meal

In my experience white wines do not improve to the same extent and you won't be far wrong if you open a white wine fifteen to thirty minutes before you sit down to the meal—later for a really good vintage wine.

What glasses do I use?

There are varying styles of glass which are all attractive. The main thing is for the glass to have a roomy bowl without being too shallow or too tall. Champagne should be served in the conventional wine glass.

How do I serve the wine?

From the right-hand side. Ladies first, of course, and remember not to fill the glasses more than two-thirds full. This allows your guests to savour the bouquet of the wine.

It is advisable to wrap the bottle in a napkin—not to hide the label of an inferior wine as some people think—but to wipe the neck of the bottle and catch any drips which might otherwise fall on the table or on one of your guests.

Decanting

All red wine which has been in bottle for a considerable time will have thrown a deposit which should under no circumstances be allowed to become mixed with the wine before it is served.

Careful decanting is therefore always necessary in the case of vintage port and sometimes with vintage clarets, Burgundies and other red wines.

This should be done at the bin in which the wine has been lying in order that the crust or sediment may not be disturbed before the wine is poured into the decanter. The bottle should be raised carefully in the same position as that in which it has been lying, and poured slowly with its neck shown up against a candle flame or other light, in order that pouring may cease immediately the sediment moves towards the opening.

The storage of wines

Ideally, wine should be stored in an underground cellar, with a well-drained concrete floor. But wherever you keep your wine, the place should always be clean and well-ventilated, dark and free from any vibrations and at a cool and even temperature away from any form of artificial heating.

An even temperature is most important and the cellar or cupboard should be maintained at about 58°F. throughout the year. White wines usually prefer a lower temperature to red and this can often be achieved by storing the white wines nearest to the floor where it is likely to be cooler.

It is absolutely essential that the cellar or cupboard should be free of draughts and strong smells. While it is in bottle the wine is 'breathing' through the cork and can thereby be contaminated by outside influences. Great care, therefore, should be taken to avoid the presence of spilt wine, mouldy straw and broken bottles.

All wine bottles should be stored on their side with the wine touching the cork and so keeping it damp and swollen to fit the neck of the bottle tightly. If possible, they should be stored in well-constructed bins with plenty of room for the air to circulate around the bottles. All straw wrappings should be removed before binning to minimize the activities of the cork weevil, and the capsules or seals of the corks should be examined from time to time. If the wine is to remain in the bins for a considerable time it is advisable to leave the tissue paper wrappers on the bottle in order to protect the labels.

Wines stored for long periods, especially vintage ports, throw a crust on the undersides of the bottle. Care should be taken to see that such wines are always stored in the same position. Labelled wines should be stored with the label uppermost and vintage port with the white-painted blaze likewise, in order to ensure that, if and when the wine is moved, the crust will always re-form in the same position.

Spirit bottles should be stored in an upright position as their contents may be adversely affected by the closures.

PRESERVES

CHUTNEYS, SAUCES AND PICKLES

It is very important to seal preserves containing vinegar very carefully. Jam-pot covers and paper covers are not sufficient to prevent evaporation of the vinegar. This means that after a few months the preserves shrink and discolour. In America melted paraffin wax, poured on top of the preserve, is used as a seal. It is an excellent way for jam too. You can wash the wax once the jar is opened and use it again melted down for the next batch of preserves.

Paraffin wax or medicated wax, as it is sometimes called, can be bought from chemists quite cheaply.

Glass jars with glass stoppers give a good seal and they look smart when on the table too. When sealing, run a finger smeared with vaseline around the stopper rim to make it quite airtight. Alternatively, use jam jars and cover with special vinegar-proof paper. All preserves should be stored in a cool dry place.

Sweet Mustard Pickle

MAKES ABOUT 8 OR 9 LB.

3 lb. cauliflower; $1\frac{1}{2}$ lb. onions, peeled and coarsely chopped; $\frac{1}{2}$ lb. green peppers, de-seeded and cut into $\frac{1}{2}$-in. pieces; 1 large cucumber, peeled; $\frac{3}{4}$ lb. cooking salt; 5 to 6 pints water; 2 oz. dry mustard; $\frac{1}{2}$ oz. turmeric; $\frac{1}{2}$ oz. ground nutmeg; $\frac{1}{2}$ oz. ground ginger; $\frac{1}{4}$ oz. curry powder; 8 oz. granulated sugar; 2 pints distilled malt vinegar; $1\frac{1}{2}$ oz. cornflour; 11-oz. can sweetcorn, drained

Preparation: 30 minutes *Cooking time: about 30 minutes*

This is a sweet version of piccalilli. First the vegetables are soaked in brine overnight, the next day the pickle is cooked.

Divide the cauliflower into small florets, discarding the stalk and leaves. This should leave about 2 lb. cauliflower. Put it into a large, deep bowl and sprinkle with some of the salt. Add the onions and peppers, sprinkling salt on each layer. Cut the cucumber in quarters lengthways, scoop out the seeds, and cut the flesh into ½-in. chunks. Add the remaining salt and pour over enough water to cover the vegetables. Press down with a heavy board so that they remain under the water, and leave overnight for at least 16 hours.

Next day drain off the liquid from the vegetables. Mix all the spices with the sugar and 1¾ pints vinegar in the preserving pan, add the prepared vegetables and simmer, covered, for 15 minutes or until they are barely tender. Blend the cornflour until smooth with the remaining vinegar.

Add a little of the hot liquid to the blended cornflour, then return it all to the pan, bring to boiling point and simmer until the mixture has thickened. Stir in the drained sweetcorn and simmer for a further 2 minutes. Pour into hot, clean jars and cover with a layer of melted paraffin wax or vinegar-proof paper.

Hot Ginger Chutney

MAKES ABOUT 4½ LB.

3 lb. ripe tomatoes, peeled; 1¼ lb. cooking apples, peeled, cored and chopped; ¾ lb. onions, peeled and chopped; 3 oz. green ginger; 1 oz. garlic, peeled; 1 level tablespoon salt; 1 pint distilled malt vinegar; 1 lb. soft brown sugar; ½ level teaspoon cayenne pepper; 1 level teaspoon ground cloves

Preparation: 30 minutes *Cooking time: about 1 hour 10 minutes*

Put the skinned tomatoes into a large pan or a preserving pan with the prepared apples and onions.

Put the green ginger into a bowl, pour over boiling water and leave for 5 minutes. Drain off the water, peel the skin from the ginger and chop the ginger finely. Chop the garlic roughly then crush it on a wooden board with the salt until no large lumps remain. Add the garlic, ginger, salt and vinegar to the pan. Cover the mixture and simmer it for about 30 minutes or until the ingredients are nearly tender, then remove the lid and continue to cook the chutney, stirring frequently, for a further 15 minutes until some of the liquid has evaporated and the mixture is a thin pulp.

Add the sugar, cayenne pepper and cloves and continue to simmer the chutney, stirring frequently, for about 25 minutes until the chutney is the correct consistency. Pour it into clean, hot jars and cover with a layer of melted paraffin wax or vinegar-proof paper.

Apricot Chutney

MAKES ABOUT 2½ LB.

1 lb. dried apricots; 1 large onion, peeled and finely chopped; 1 level tablespoon cooking salt; ¾ lb. demerara sugar; 3 oz. seedless raisins, each cut in half if large; ½ pint distilled malt vinegar; 1 oz. whole pickling spices

Preparation: 30 minutes *Cooking time: about 1 hour*

Being made from dried apricots this can be made at any time of year. This recipe is very good though expensive to make.

Leave the apricots to soak in a bowl of cold water for at least 6 hours, or overnight. Drain the fruit, cut each apricot in half and put them in a pan with the onion, salt, sugar, raisins and vinegar. Tie the pickling spice in a piece of muslin and add this to the pan. Bring the mixture to boiling point, cover the pan and simmer the contents gently for 50 minutes, stirring occasionally so that it does not stick. Remove the lid and continue to simmer the chutney for a further 10 minutes, or until thick, stirring frequently.

Remove the bag of pickling spice from the pan and pour the chutney into clean, hot jars. Cover with a layer of melted paraffin wax or vinegar-proof paper.

Red Tomato Chutney

MAKES ABOUT 6½ LB.

9 lb. ripe, firm tomatoes; 1 lb. onions, peeled and finely chopped; 6 cloves garlic, crushed; ½ pint distilled malt vinegar; 1 oz. dry mustard; 1½ oz. salt; 1 level teaspoon mixed spice; ½ level teaspoon cayenne pepper; 1 level teaspoon paprika pepper; 1½ lb. granulated sugar.

Preparation: 35 minutes *Cooking time: about 1¼ hours*

First skin the tomatoes. Dip the tomatoes, a few at a time, into boiling water. Immerse them for about 10 seconds then drain them and turn them into the bowl of cold water. Then remove them from the cold water and peel off the skins. Chop the tomatoes coarsely and put them into a large saucepan or a preserving pan with the onion and garlic. Simmer the tomato mixture for about 15 minutes, stirring frequently, until it turns into a thick pulp.

Add the vinegar, mustard, salt, mixed spice, cayenne pepper and paprika pepper to the pan, stir well and continue to simmer the mixture for about half an hour until it is thick. Care must be taken not to let the mixture burn, so it should be stirred frequently. When the mixture is thick stir in the sugar and cook the chutney, without simmering, over a low heat until the sugar has completely dissolved. Then increase the heat and simmer the chutney for a further 20 minutes or until it is thick, stirring constantly.

Have ready the clean, hot, dry jars and pour the hot chutney into them. Cover with a layer of melted paraffin wax or vinegar-proof paper.

Betty's Green Tomato Chutney

MAKES ABOUT 8 LB. CHUTNEY

2 lb. green tomatoes, chopped; 3 pints vinegar (distilled malt); 3 cooking apples (windfalls will do), peeled and chopped; 2 lb. onions, peeled and finely chopped; 1 lb. seedless raisins; 1 lb. 6 oz. soft brown sugar; 2 oz. dried root ginger; 1½ oz. mustard seed; 1 level tablespoon salt; 1 level teaspoon cayenne pepper

Preparation: 30 minutes *Cooking time: about 1 hour*

When home-grown tomatoes have failed to ripen this is an excellent chutney for using them up.

Put the tomatoes into a pan with half the vinegar and simmer them until they are soft. Sieve the mixture. Return this purée to the pan with the apples, onions, raisins, sugar and remaining vinegar. Tie the ginger in a piece of muslin with the mustard seed and add it to the pan with the salt and cayenne pepper. Bring it to boiling point and simmer it gently with the lid off the pan for about half to three-quarters of an hour until it is a fairly thick pulp. Squeeze the juices out of the spice bag into the chutney. Pour the chutney into clean, hot jars and cover it with a layer of melted paraffin wax or vinegar-proof paper.

Tomato Mustard Relish

MAKES ABOUT 4½ LB.

1 lb. tomatoes; 2 green peppers; 1 lb. onions, peeled and finely chopped; 1 lb. cooking apples, cored and finely chopped; 2 cloves garlic, crushed; ½ pint distilled malt vinegar; 12 oz. granulated sugar; 1 level tablespoon salt; 1 level tablespoon paprika pepper; ½ level teaspoon cayenne pepper; 1 level tablespoon made mustard; ½ level teaspoon mixed spice; 5-oz. can tomato purée

Preparation: 30 minutes *Cooking time: about 40 minutes*

This is a good family chutney. Adding tomato purée concentrate gives not only tomato flavour cheaply but also a pleasant colour.

Dip the tomatoes in boiling water for about 10 seconds then put them into a bowl of cold water to cool. Remove the skins and discard them then chop the flesh and put it into a bowl. Cut the pepper in half, remove the stalk and seeds then chop the flesh very finely and add it to the tomato with the prepared onions, apples and garlic. Put all the prepared ingredients into a pan with the vinegar, cover the pan and simmer the mixture for about 30 minutes, stirring occasionally, or until the mixture is tender.

Add all the other ingredients to the pan and boil the relish, stirring frequently, until fairly thick, for about 5 minutes. Put the relish into clean, dry jars and cover it with a layer of melted paraffin wax or with vinegar-proof paper.

Spiced Tomato Ketchup

MAKES ABOUT 3 PINTS

5 lb. ripe tomatoes, quartered; ½ lb. onions, peeled and coarsely chopped; 3 cloves garlic, peeled and chopped; ¾ oz. dry mustard; ½ pint distilled malt vinegar; ¾ lb. granulated sugar; ¾ oz. salt; 1 level teaspoon mixed spice; ½ level teaspoon cayenne pepper

Preparation: 40 minutes *Cooking time: about 1 hour*

Put the tomatoes, onions and garlic into a large pan, cover the pan and simmer the contents over a low heat for about 20 minutes or until the onion is tender. Stir occasionally so that the mixture does not stick to the pan.

Rub the tomato mixture through a fine sieve into a bowl. Rinse out the pan. Put the mustard in the pan and blend with a little of the vinegar. Add the rest of the vinegar with the sugar, salt, mixed spice and cayenne pepper. Heat it gently until the sugar has dissolved, boil the mixture for about 10 minutes until it is the consistency of a pouring sauce and coats the back of a spoon lightly. Stir frequently.

Pour the sauce into hot, clean bottles and fill to within 1 in. of the tops. Cork with boiled, new corks, tying them on loosely with string to allow for expansion while they are being processed. As ripe tomato and mushroom sauces are liable to ferment during storage it is best to sterilize them after filling the bottles. To do this put the bottles into a large pan. Fill this with cold water up to the necks of the bottles, bring the water to boiling point and simmer for 20 minutes. Remove the bottles from the water. Press down the corks into the bottles. When the bottles have cooled either screw on caps or dip the last ½ in. of the bottle neck into melted paraffin wax to give an airtight seal.

Spiced Pickled Peaches

MAKES ABOUT 8 LB.

4 lb. granulated sugar; 1 qt. distilled malt vinegar; thinly peeled rind of 1 lemon; ½ oz. cloves; ½ oz. allspice; ¼ oz. root ginger; ¼ oz. cinnamon stick; 8 lb. firm peaches

Preparation: 30 minutes *Cooking time: about 35 minutes*

Spiced peaches go well with boiled bacon or ham. They also go well with cold cuts of chicken and turkey. Pears may also be preserved in this way.

Put the sugar into a preserving pan with the vinegar and leave it to dissolve over a low heat. Put the lemon rind, cloves, allspice, ginger and cinnamon sticks into a piece of muslin, tie it with string to form a bag and add it to the pan.

Peel the peaches, cut in halves and remove the stones and drop them into a weak salt and water solution to prevent them going brown. When they are all prepared rinse them in cold water and add them to the pan. Cover the pan and simmer the peaches very gently for about 20 to 30 minutes until they are tender. Do not allow them to cook too quickly or they will break up.

When the peaches are tender drain them and arrange neatly in jars. Boil the liquid rapidly for about 5 minutes until it is the consistency of thin syrup, then pour it over the peaches, while it is still hot. Cover the jars with a layer of melted paraffin wax or vinegar-proof paper.

Leave the peaches to mature for at least 3 months before using.

Quince Jelly

MAKES ABOUT 5½ LB.

3 lb. quinces; 4½ pints water; sugar

Preparation: 20 minutes *Cooking time: about 2 hours*

If the fruit is fully ripe add ½ oz. citric or tartaric acid to help obtain a good set.

Cut the quinces into fairly small pieces and put them into a preserving pan or saucepan with 3 pints of the water. Cover the pan and simmer the contents for about 1 hour, or until they are tender.

Pour boiling water through a jelly bag or thick linen cloth, suspend the jelly bag or cloth in a suitable place and tip the fruit into it. Allow it to drain for about half an hour, or until there is little liquid draining from it. Do not push the fruit juice through the bag by force.

Return the remaining pulp to the pan with the rest of the water. The citric or tartaric acid, if used, should be added at this stage, blended with 1 tablespoon water. Simmer the fruit for 30 minutes then pour it into the jelly bag and leave it to drain for 1 hour. Again, do not push the pulp through the bag, otherwise the jelly will be cloudy. Mix the two extracts together and measure the quantity. There should be about 3 pints. Test the extract for pectin content (see note below) and then return it to the pan with the sugar. Stir the preserve over a low heat until the sugar has completely dissolved, then bring it to boiling point and boil it rapidly until setting point (220°F.) is reached. Pour the jelly into clean, hot jam jars, having first removed any scum from the jelly with a spoon, then cover the jelly with either a layer of melted paraffin wax or a jam-pot cover.

TO TEST THE EXTRACT FOR PECTIN: Take 1 teaspoon of the strained extract and put it into a small bowl with 3 teaspoons methylated spirit. If the pectin clots well, up to 1¼ lb. sugar may be added to each pint of juice. If there is a poor clot only ¾ lb. sugar should be added to each pint of liquid. An average amount is 1 lb. sugar to each pint of liquid.

Whole Strawberry Jam

MAKES ABOUT 5 LB.

2¼ lb. small firm strawberries; 3 tablespoons lemon juice; 3 lb. granulated sugar; ½ bottle Certo (commercial pectin)

Preparation: 15 minutes *Cooking time: about 15 minutes*

This strawberry jam has an excellent colour and sets well. Using small strawberries means that with each spoonful of jam there are at least a couple of strawberries.

Remove the stalks from the strawberries. Do not wash the fruit unless it is very dirty but put it into the preserving pan and sprinkle the sugar on top. Leave it to stand for one hour, stirring occasionally. Put the pan over a low heat and stir occasionally until the sugar has dissolved completely. Add a small knob of butter to the pan to reduce the scum. Bring the jam to a full rolling boil and boil it rapidly for 4 minutes, stirring occasionally. Remove the pan from the heat and stir in the Certo. Leave the jam to cool for at least 20 to 30 minutes to prevent the fruit rising to the tops of the jars.

Pour the jam into clean, hot jars and cover and label it in the usual way.

Lemon Curd

MAKES 1 LB.

4 oz. butter; 8 oz. caster sugar; 2 large lemons; 2 large eggs

Preparation: 15 minutes *Cooking time: about 20 minutes*

This sharp lemon curd keeps for a month in the refrigerator.

Put the butter and sugar in the top part of a double boiler with boiling water in the lower part, or in a basin over a pan of boiling water, and stir until the butter has melted. Mix the finely grated lemon rind with the eggs in a bowl then squeeze the juice from the lemons and strain it on to the eggs and lemon rind. Add this mixture to the butter and sugar in the pan and cook it over the hot, but not boiling, water until the mixture thickens sufficiently to coat the back of a wooden spoon.

Pour it into a clean, hot, 1-lb. jam jar or several small jars and cover it in the usual way.

Charlcombe Farm Mincemeat

MAKES ABOUT 5 LB.

1½ lb. stoned raisins, minced or chopped finely; ¾ lb. currants; ½ lb. sultanas; ¼ lb. candied peel, finely chopped; ½ lb. cooking apples, peeled, cored and minced or chopped; 6 oz. shredded suet; ½ level teaspoon mixed spice; grated rind and juice of 2 lemons; 1 lb. soft brown sugar; 6 tablespoons brandy, rum or sherry

Preparation: 30 minutes

Mincemeat is not cheap to make at home unless you have a free source of apples but it is so good it's worth it. Lace it with brandy, sherry or rum if you like. This mincemeat is an excellent keeper. Adding an extra pound of apples makes it more economical, although of course it does not keep as well. But with a large family wanting lots of mince pies it is the answer! Alternatively, add cooked apple purée or sieved apple to home-made or bought mincemeat at the time of baking to make it go further.

Wash the dried fruit and leave to dry. Put the peel, apple, suet, spice, lemon rind and juice and the sugar into a bowl. Add the prepared fruit and finally the brandy, rum or sherry. Mix well, then cover the bowl with a cloth and leave the mincemeat to stand overnight. Next day turn it into clean, dry jars and cover and label in the usual way.

Seville Orange Marmalade

MAKES ABOUT 10 LB.

3 lb. Seville oranges; 6 pints water; 6 lb. granulated sugar (or

4 lb. granulated sugar and 2 lb. Barbados sugar); a knob of butter; the juice of 2 lemons
N.B. If you prefer a dark marmalade use Barbados sugar in the quantity given above.

Preparation: 30 minutes *Cooking time: about 2 hours 20 minutes*

Wash and dry the fruit and cut it in half. Squeeze out the juice and put it into the preserving pan. Put the pips into a muslin bag and add this to the preserving pan. Shred the peel fairly finely and add this to the juice and pips with the water. Simmer the mixture gently for at least two hours, stirring frequently, until the peel is really tender and the liquid has reduced by almost half.

Remove the bag of pips from the pan and squeeze any liquid from it into the pan. Blend in the sugar, and cook the marmalade slowly, without allowing it to simmer, until the sugar has dissolved, then bring the marmalade to boiling point and boil it rapidly until setting point is reached (220°F.). Add a small knob of butter to the marmalade at this stage as this helps to reduce the scum. Remove the pan from the heat and leave the marmalade for about 10 minutes to cool slightly. Then stir it once more to distribute the peel cleanly and pour it into clean, hot jars. Cover and label in the usual way.

Charlcombe Farm Minced Peel Marmalade

MAKES 14 LB.

3 lb. bitter Seville oranges; 2 lemons; 7 pints water; 8 lb. granulated sugar

Preparation: 30 minutes *Cooking time: about 2 hours 20 minutes*

Wash the fruit then cut in half and squeeze out the juice and put juice in a preserving or large pan. Cut the fruit skin into quarters then using a knife cut away the white pith and flesh, put this and the pips in a piece of muslin and tie with string to form a bag.

Using a coarse blade, mince the peel into the large saucepan containing the juice. Put in the muslin bag and tie the end of the string to one of the handles of the pan. Add the water and bring slowly to the boil. Simmer gently for 2 hours until the peel is tender and the contents of the pan have reduced by half. Add the sugar. Stir over low heat until sugar has dissolved, bring up to the boil and cook rapidly until setting point is reached—about 20 minutes (220°F.).

Draw the pan off the heat, cool for 10–15 minutes, then pour into hot, clean, dry jars. Cover and label in the usual way.

Red House Dark Coarse-Cut Marmalade

MAKES ABOUT 9 LB.

2 lb. Seville oranges; 1 lemon; 7 pints water; 6 lb. granulated sugar; 2 level tablespoons black treacle

Preparation: 30 minutes *Cooking time: about 2 hours 20 minutes*

The treacle in this marmalade gives it a deep golden colour without excessive boiling, which is the usual way, and which is inclined to make a thinly set marmalade which slips off the toast!

Wash the fruit, cut it in half and squeeze out the juice. Remove as much of the pith as possible and place it in a muslin bag with the pips. Shred the peel fairly finely. Put it into a preserving pan or large saucepan with the muslin bag, juice and water. Bring to the boil and simmer gently for about 2 hours, or until it is reduced by half and the peel is tender.

Remove the bag of pips, squeeze it gently to remove any pectin. Add the sugar and treacle and heat very gently, without boiling, until the sugar has dissolved completely. Bring to boiling point and then boil rapidly until setting point is reached (220°F.). Remove the pan from the heat and allow the marmalade to stand for 5–10 minutes. Have ready clean, hot jam jars and fill the jars almost to the top with marmalade. Cover and label in the usual way.

Vanilla Butter Fudge

MAKES 1 LB.

$\frac{1}{4}$ pint (small tin) evaporated milk; 3 oz. butter; 1 lb. granulated sugar; $\frac{1}{4}$ pint water; $\frac{1}{4}$ teaspoon vanilla essence

Preparation: 15 minutes *Cooking time: about 30 minutes*

Get out a 7-in. square tin, lightly buttered.

If you are making a couple of pounds do it in two separate sessions as it is easier to manage this way.

Put the milk, butter, sugar and water into a large, heavy-based pan. Stir it once or twice to mix all the ingredients together once the butter has melted, then leave the pan over a very low heat until the sugar has dissolved. This will take some time and the mixture must not be allowed to boil at all while the sugar is dissolving. Brush the sides of the pan occasionally with a brush dipped in warm water to remove any sugar crystals which may have formed. When the sugar has completely dissolved bring the fudge to boiling point then boil it steadily to a temperature of 238°F., if you have a sugar thermometer, or until a little of the mixture dropped into a bowl of cold water will form a soft ball. Stir the fudge from time to time to prevent its burning (it will be particularly likely to catch just before it is ready). When the fudge has reached the required temperature remove the pan from the heat, add essence, leave for a few moments to cool, then beat the fudge until it is a thick, creamy consistency and pour it into the prepared tin. When it is just firm mark the fudge into squares with a sharp knife. Cut it into pieces when it is completely set.

Rum Truffles

MAKES 30 SMALL BALLS

4 oz. plain chocolate, broken into small pieces; 2 oz. butter; 1 egg yolk, beaten; about 1 tablespoon apricot jam; about 2 tablespoons rum; 6 oz. icing sugar, sifted; 4 oz. (8) digestive biscuits, crushed, or crumbled sponge or Madeira cake; 2 oz. raisins, chopped

For coating: chocolate vermicelli

Preparation: 20 minutes *Cooking time: about 15 minutes*

Although this is a precise recipe don't hesitate to adapt it to the ingredients that you have on hand. When almond paste or cake icings are left over, mash them down and add with more apricot jam to make a manageable rolling mixture.

Put the chocolate into a bowl over a pan of hot water with the butter. When it has melted stir in the egg yolk and then remove the bowl from the pan. Work in the jam, rum, icing sugar, biscuit crumbs and raisins. Turn on to a tin plate, cover and leave in the refrigerator or other cold place for at least a couple of hours to harden then roll it into about 30 small balls. Coat the balls with chocolate vermicelli and leave them overnight to harden.

CELEBRATIONS

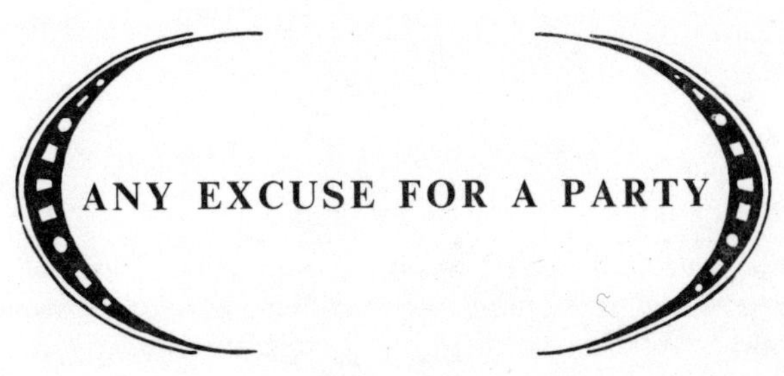

ANY EXCUSE FOR A PARTY

One might say that dinner parties, entertaining friends in small numbers, are chicken feed compared with a larger party which one has just once in a while, whether it be a housewarming, drinks, or family celebration. But once you sit down and get a few ideas on paper everything is much easier. The more detailed and thorough the planning the surer you are to be relaxed and easy on the day. Get ahead as much as you can with the preparations, leaving as little to do just beforehand as possible.

DRINKS PARTY EATS

I loathe hoards of little bits on toast coated in aspic which take ages to make and to my mind are not worth the effort. I would much rather make the selection small but the quality tops, say, four kinds of savouries, two hot and two cold. When the guests arrive give them the cold ones plus the usual nuts and crisps, then as the party progresses bring on the hot savouries straight from the oven where they have been keeping warm.

BUFFETS

As few of us have enough chairs or indeed a table at which to seat a crowd, a party buffet style is the answer. If you have not enough plates and cutlery, you can beg or borrow some or even use the very smart disposable ones which adorn the more elegant picnic displays in stores. If you plan a cold buffet give everyone a cup of hot soup to start with to cheer them on their way. A selection of ready-sliced cold roast meats, turkey, chicken or ham plus some cold sausages is a good choice—remember to slice the meat into manageable pieces so that they may be easily eaten with a fork. Freshly baked pork pie, sliced, is excellent if specially ordered, then you will be sure to have crisp pastry. Serve with pickles and large bowls of salad. For the hungry young, have plenty of hunks of crisp French bread and butter. For a more sophisticated cold buffet main dish try spiced creamed chicken (see page 108).

Hot dishes go down well. Something like Lasagne, a delicious Italian pasta dish made in large oven-to-table dishes (see page 103) and served with green salad. Casseroles are suitable too. If you are hard up and want a hearty main dish, Nasi Goreng just fills the bill (see page 96).

A classic trifle or fresh fruit salad is a natural thought for dessert. These are some more original spectacular ideas. Cut a pineapple in half lengthways, including the green top. Scoop out and chop up flesh, discard core, fill shell with fresh fruit salad including the pineapple pieces and a little kirsch. Serve extra fruit salad in a glass bowl. Raspberry meringue is always popular (see page 138).

CHILDREN'S BIRTHDAY PARTIES

I have come to the conclusion it is best to ask the children themselves what kind of party food they would like. There seems little point in making masses of jellies, little cakes, animal sandwiches and numerous confections when all they often want are chocolate crispies, chocolate finger biscuits, crisps, sausages, grown-up savouries and ice-cream. I find the birthday cake seems the all-important part for small ones. A train made from sponge squares and a Swiss roll for the engine body, biscuits for the wheels, is a favourite. An igloo made from a Victoria sandwich sponge base baked in a pudding basin, cut in layers and filled with lemon butter icing, then covered all over with white marshmallows built carefully round the outside, fixed with jam or icing is also popular. Arrange around the edge penguins or other animals, and trees. Children of all ages like a present to take home; this can give decoration to the cake, for example little gold bags of chocolate money or small bags of Smarties around the cake. Boys could have a cake decorated with miniature cars and ships. Do not forget candles. For most ages they are a must.

CHRISTENING PARTY

Depending upon the time of day, the christening party could be either a cold buffet lunch, a help-yourself affair (see page 191) or afternoon tea plus champagne or whatever is chosen to drink the health of the new offspring. The cake may be either a rich fruit cake like the Christmas cake recipe on page 217 or a light sponge which is a far more suitable choice for children to enjoy as well as grown-ups. The icing, either pink or blue, need not be elaborate.

Christening Cake

7 oz. self-raising flour; 2 oz. cornflour; 9 large eggs; 9 oz. caster sugar; 4 tablespoons salad oil

For the butter cream filling: 6 oz. unsalted butter; 12 oz. icing sugar, sifted; about 3 tablespoons lemon juice; 8 oz. crystallized pineapple, finely chopped

Almond paste: 1½ lb. almond paste; 3 tablespoons apricot jam, sieved

For the icing: 4 egg whites; 2 lb. icing sugar, sifted; 1 tablespoon lemon juice; water; pink or blue colouring

For decoration: 1 yard ¼-in. wide deep pink or blue ribbon; 2 yards ¼-in. pink or blue ribbon; 1½ yards frilled white lace; stork; 12 in. silver cake board

Preparation: 1½ hours *Cooking time: about 1 hour*

Get out a 10-in. cake tin, greased and lined.

Set oven at 350°F., Gas 4.

Sift together the flour and cornflour. Place the eggs and sugar in a bowl and stand the bowl over a pan of hot water. Whisk until the mixture is pale in colour and the whisk leaves a trail when removed from the mixture. Remove the bowl from the heat and whisk for a further 2–3 minutes. Alternatively beat the mixture in an electric mixer until the same result is obtained. Fold in the flour alternately with the oil, using a metal spoon. The flour and oil should be folded in very lightly so that no air is knocked out of the mixture. Turn it into the prepared cake tin and bake for about 50–60 minutes or until the centre of the cake springs back when lightly pressed. Remove from the oven, leave to cool in the tin for about 5 minutes then turn out to cool on a wire rack. When the cake is completely cold it may be filled and decorated.

PREPARE THE FILLING: Cream the butter until soft, beat in the sugar well, add the lemon juice and crystallized pineapple.

Cut the cake horizontally into three layers then sandwich them together again with the filling.

PREPARE THE ALMOND PASTE: Roll it out on a sugared board. Use half of the paste to form a 10 in. circle. Roll the remainder into a long strip the depth and circumference of the cake. Brush the top and sides of the cake with the jam then press the almond paste firmly into position.

PREPARE THE ICING: Whisk the egg whites in a bowl until they are frothy then whisk in the icing sugar a tablespoon at a time, whisking well after each addition. When about half the icing sugar has been added stir in the lemon juice then beat in the remaining icing sugar with a wooden spoon. Set aside about 4 heaped tablespoons of the icing and keep it covered with a damp cloth or in an airtight container.

Thin down the remaining, larger portion, of icing with lemon juice until it is the consistency of a thick glacé icing. Colour it pink or pale blue with a few drops of pink or blue colouring. Place the cake on a wire cake rack and pour the icing over the cake to cover it completely. Smooth out the sides with a palette knife if necessary then bang the cake rack gently up and down to coat the cake evenly and to remove any air bubbles in the icing.

Leave the cake overnight or until completely dry then carefully remove it from the wire rack and arrange on the silver board. With a shell pipe and some of the remaining icing pipe a shell pattern round the top of the cake. Pipe small dots underneath the shell edging using a plain writing pipe. Write on the cake the child's name, date, etc.

Thread the thin pink or blue ribbon through the lace edging and secure the lace to the bottom of the cake with pins. Use the wide ribbon and remaining lace to make a rosette and place it on the front of the cake. Put the stork on top of the cake and tie a bow of the thin pink or blue ribbon on to the baby's cradle which the stork is carrying.

A DIFFERENT KIND OF SUPPER PARTY— A FONDUE PARTY

Having friends in for a fondue party is a fun idea; not only does it make sure that you, the hostess, enjoy yourself but it keeps your friends busy cooking their own supper. Once they get the hang of the idea they will enjoy dabbling in the various sauces as they do in Switzerland and Austria. For Fondue Bourguignonne you fry cubes of tender steak in oil on skewers then serve with a selection of sauces and salads too. No need for potatoes, just serve crisp French bread and plenty of butter.

If you haven't a smart fondue set and can't beg or borrow one, use a little calor gas stove or, failing this, a picnic spirit heater. It is best to heat the pan containing the oil (you will need about 2 in. of oil in the pan) on the hob of the cooker in the kitchen until a faint haze is rising then transfer it to the fondue stove. If you have more than six guests you will, ideally, need two pans being heated by a shuttle system from the kitchen. Remember when heating up the oil that it will heat up quicker with a lid on the pan but keep an eye on it because it should not become too hot. When the guests are cooking their meat cubes mark their skewers with coloured tape or wools so that they know which is theirs. If using metal skewers or forks be sure to cool them before popping the meat in the mouth.

COOKING THE MEAT

Keep the oil hot by returning it to the cooker at intervals and not cooking more than eight lots of meat at the same time. Your guests will time their own steak cubes, some will like them rarer than others. For six people allow from 6–8 oz. rump steak per person and about 1 pint salad or corn oil.

MAKING THE SAUCES

These can all be made beforehand. If you haven't time to make them all buy a chunky tomato chutney instead of making the Provençal sauce.

TO DRINK

A warming hot punch—Glühwein as this is called in the mountains. Lace it with cheap brandy if your drinks cupboard will stand it.

If you prefer a cheese fondue this is a classic one:

Cheese Fondue

FOR 4

1 clove of garlic, peeled; ½ lb. Swiss Emmenthal cheese; ½ lb. Swiss Gruyère cheese; 4 glasses dry white wine; 1 oz. cornflour; salt; pepper; 1 tablespoon kirsch

Preparation: 10 minutes *Cooking time: about 25 minutes*

Crush the garlic very finely and grate the cheese. Pour all but about 3 tablespoons of the wine into a thick pan, add the garlic and cheese and heat the mixture very slowly until all the cheese has dissolved. Do not allow it to boil. Blend the cornflour with the remainder of the wine in a bowl until it is smooth. Add a little of the hot cheese mixture to the cornflour then return it to the pan—as when making custard. Carefully bring the fondue to the boil, stirring all the time until the mixture has thickened. Add salt and pepper to taste, stir in the kirsch and serve at once.

Chicory Salad

FOR 6 WITH SPROUT SLAW

¾ lb. tomatoes; 1 green pepper; 4 small heads of chicory; 2 tablespoons salad oil; 1 tablespoon wine vinegar; ½ level teaspoon salt; ½ level teaspoon caster sugar; ⅛ level teaspoon freshly ground black pepper; ½ level teaspoon French mustard; 1 medium onion, peeled and very finely chopped

Preparation: 15 minutes

Put the tomatoes into boiling water for ten seconds then place them in a bowl of cold water until they are cool enough to handle. Cut the green pepper in half and remove the stem and seeds. Grill the halves for about 3–5 minutes, skin side uppermost, until the skin is pale brown and the pepper is softened. Peel off the skin and leave the pepper to cool then cut it into ¼-in. strips. Peel and quarter the tomatoes and remove the seeds. Split the chicory heads lengthwise into 6 pieces. Blend together the oil, vinegar, salt, sugar, pepper and mustard in a bowl. Sprinkle in the onion then put in the other salad ingredients haphazardly. Do not toss the salad in the dressing in the bowl until five minutes before it is served.

Sprout Slaw

FOR 6 WITH CHICORY SALAD

½ lb. sprouts; 4 oz. cooked ham, diced; 8-oz. can pineapple pieces, drained; 1 eating apple, cored and cut into small cubes; 8 tablespoons mayonnaise; 1 level teaspoon made mustard; 2 teaspoons wine vinegar; 1 tablespoon salad oil; ground black pepper; salt; sprigs of watercress

Preparation: 15 minutes

Remove the outer leaves from the sprouts, cut the sprouts in quarters and remove the thickest part of the stem then shred the leaves finely. Put them into a large bowl with the ham, pineapple and apple. In another bowl mix together the mayonnaise, mustard, vinegar, oil, pepper and salt. Pour this mixture into the large bowl and mix thoroughly, adding extra seasoning if necessary. To serve garnish with sprigs of watercress.

THE SAUCES

Cold Spiced Mushroom Sauce

FOR 6 WITH THE OTHER SAUCES

6 tablespoons salad oil; 2 tablespoons wine vinegar; 1 teaspoon chopped capers; 1 teaspoon chopped gherkin; 1 teaspoon chopped

parsley; 1 teaspoon chopped chives or very finely chopped onion; 2 level teaspoons tomato purée; pinch dried tarragon or chervil; salt; pepper; ¼ lb. button mushrooms, washed, dried and finely sliced

Preparation: 10 minutes

Put all the ingredients except the mushrooms into a screw-topped jar and shake them thoroughly until they are well amalgamated. At least an hour before serving add the prepared mushrooms and leave them to marinade in the mixture. To serve, turn the mixture out into a small bowl.

Hot Provençal Sauce

FOR 6 WITH THE OTHER SAUCES

1 lb. ripe tomatoes; 2 tablespoons salad oil; 1 Spanish onion, peeled and finely chopped; 1 clove garlic; salt; pepper; 1 tablespoon vinegar; 1 teaspoon sugar; ¼ level teaspoon dried basil; 1 teaspoon chopped parsley

Preparation: 15 minutes *Cooking time: about 15 minutes*

Put the tomatoes into boiling water for 10 seconds then remove them and put them into a bowl of cold water. When they have cooled sufficiently remove and discard the skins. Cut the tomatoes in quarters, remove the seeds and chop the flesh. Heat the oil in a pan and fry the onion with the whole clove of garlic until the onion is soft and transparent. Add the chopped tomato and continue to cook until the tomato has formed a purée. Remove the clove of garlic and stir in the seasoning, vinegar, sugar, basil and parsley. Turn into a small bowl and serve, preferably hot, but it may be served cold.

Sweet 'n Sour Mustard and Dill Sauce

FOR 6 WITH THE OTHER SAUCES

4 level tablespoons caster sugar; 2 tablespoons wine vinegar; 2 tablespoons salad oil; 2 level tablespoons French mustard; ½ level teaspoon dried dill; salt; pepper

Preparation: 5 minutes *Cooking time: about 15 minutes*

Put the sugar and vinegar into a small saucepan and leave it over a gentle heat until the sugar has dissolved. If necessary brush the sides of the pan with cold water to dissolve any crystals of sugar. Bring the syrup to boiling point and simmer it until it has reduced by about one-third. Remove the pan from the heat, allow it to cool a little then blend in the salad oil, mustard, dill and plenty of salt and pepper. Pour the sauce into a small bowl and serve cold.

Curried Mayonnaise

FOR 6 WITH THE OTHER SAUCES

2 eggs; $\frac{1}{4}$ pint mayonnaise (preferably home-made); 3 teaspoons lemon juice; 1 level teaspoon curry powder; 1 heaped teaspoon mango chutney; salt; freshly-ground black pepper

Preparation: 10 minutes *Cooking time: about 12 minutes*

Boil the eggs in water for 12 minutes then leave them in cold water until they are completely cold before removing the shells. Meanwhile mix together the mayonnaise, lemon juice, curry powder, mango chutney, salt and plenty of freshly-ground black pepper. Chop the hard-boiled eggs coarsely and stir them into the mayonnaise. Turn the mayonnaise into a small bowl to serve.

Glühwein

FOR 6

2 lemons; 1 bottle cheap red wine, e.g. Spanish Burgundy; 1 pint water; 8 cloves; 1 stick cinnamon; 2–4 oz. caster sugar; sherry glass of cheap brandy, if liked

Preparation: 10 minutes *Cooking time: about 1 hour*

Peel the zest very thinly from the lemons, cut a few slices of lemon for garnish then squeeze the remaining lemons to extract the juice. Put the lemon zest, juice, wine, water, cloves and cinnamon into a pan, put on the lid, bring the Glühwein to just below simmering point and leave it at this temperature for one hour or more. Lift out the lemon rind, cloves and cinnamon and add sugar to taste. Serve hot with lemon slices floating on top. Add the brandy just before serving if a more potent drink is favoured.

DRINKS PARTY TEMPTERS

Hot Kidney and Bacon Kebabs

MAKES 30

5 lambs' kidneys; 10 rashers (about 5 oz.) streaky bacon; 3 oz. button mushrooms; 30 wooden cocktail sticks; salad oil

Preparation: 20 minutes *Cooking time: about 30 minutes*

These are a bit of an effort to make but can be easily made ahead and reheated. They always seem to be the most popular of all the hot eats that I make, especially with the men.

Remove the fat and membrane from the kidneys. Cut each kidney in half and remove the core with a pair of scissors. Cut each kidney into six pieces. Remove the rinds from the bacon rashers, stretch the rashers on a wooden board with the back of a knife then cut each in three. Roll up each small piece of bacon to form a roll. Wash and dry the mushrooms, remove a little of the stem then cut each mushroom in half.

Assemble the kebabs with a piece of kidney, a bacon roll and half a mushroom on each cocktail stick. Place on a baking sheet, brush with oil and grill for about 5 minutes. Turn the kebabs over and grill on the other side. Arrange in a serving dish and serve hot, with crisps piled on the dish too.

Baby Quiches

MAKES 20

8 oz. plain flour; ½ level teaspoon salt; 2 oz. butter; 2 oz. lard; about 8 teaspoons water.

For the filling: 5 rashers streaky bacon, de-rinded; 2 oz. cheese, grated; 2 eggs, blended; 6 tablespoons milk; 1 teaspoon chopped parsley; salt; pepper

Preparation: 25 minutes *Cooking time: about 45 minutes*

You will need 20 shallow patty tins, greased.

Set oven at 375°F., Gas 5.

Sift the flour and salt into a bowl. Cut the fats into small pieces then rub them into the flour until the mixture resembles fine breadcrumbs. Add enough of the water to mix to a fairly stiff dough. Roll out thinly on a floured board and cut into 20 circles with a 3-in. plain cutter. Line the patty tins with the circles, prick well, place a piece of greaseproof paper or crumpled foil inside each and, if using paper, fill with baking beans. Bake for 15 minutes. Remove the patty tins from the oven and take out the beans and paper or foil.

Meanwhile fry the bacon without any extra fat over a gentle heat for about 2 minutes. Drain the rashers on kitchen paper then cut into small pieces. Divide the bacon and cheese between the pastry cases. Blend together the eggs, milk, parsley and seasoning. Divide between the pastry cases.

Reduce the oven temperature to 325°F., Gas 3 and bake for about 15–20 minutes or until the filling is just firm to the touch. Cool on a wire rack or serve hot.

Asparagus Rolls

MAKES 40

2 small brown Hovis loaves, preferably 2 days old; 5 oz. butter; two 10-oz. cans asparagus, drained

Preparation: 35 minutes

Cut 40 slices of bread and butter, making each slice wafer thin. Remove the crusts with a sharp knife. Place a piece of asparagus diagonally on a slice of bread, then roll up the bread very carefully so that a corner of the bread is on top. Prepare the remaining rolls in the same way. Wrap the asparagus rolls in damp greaseproof paper, then foil, so that they are completely covered, then put them in the refrigerator or other cool place until required.

Smoked Salmon and Crab Rolls

FOR 24 ROLLS

1 small brown loaf, sliced; 2½ oz. butter; ¾ lb. smoked salmon, thinly sliced; 6-oz. can crab; 2 tablespoons good mayonnaise; lemon juice; salt; freshly-ground black pepper; 1 punnet cress; 1 lemon

Preparation: 35 minutes

These are definitely in the luxury class.

Butter twelve slices of bread, remove the crusts and cut each slice in two. Cut the smoked salmon into about 24 small, even-sized pieces. Drain the crab and flake it, removing any membrane. Mix the flakes with the mayonnaise and add enough lemon juice, salt and pepper to season really well. Place a small amount of the crab on each piece of salmon, and roll up the pieces firmly. Garnish each finger of bread with a little cress, place a salmon roll on top, and sprinkle it with lemon juice and pepper. Decorate each finger with a tiny lemon wedge, and keep rolls covered until required.

Avocado Dip

FOR 10

4 ripe avocado pears; ¼ pint double cream; 3-oz. packet cream-cheese spread; ½ level teaspoon made mustard; 4 level teaspoons caster sugar; 2 tablespoons lemon juice; 1 teaspoon cider vinegar; salt; pepper; green colouring; watercress

Preparation: 10 minutes

This is best made on the day it is needed as it discolours if kept too long.

Cut the avocadoes in half, remove the stones and scoop out the flesh. Mash the flesh in a bowl with a fork until smooth. Blend together the cream and cream cheese then stir this into the avocado mixture, or put all the ingredients in a blender. Season with the mustard, sugar, lemon juice, cider vinegar and plenty of salt and pepper. Add a few drops of green colouring if necessary.

Pile into a dish and serve with crisps, cauliflower florets, carrot sticks and leaves of chicory. Garnish with a sprig of watercress.

CATERING FOR A CROWD

Catering for a number of guests is often quite a problem as it is not something one is tackling every day. Here is a check list guide so that you can, with the aid of a pencil and paper and a spot of arithmetic, work out just how much food to buy and how far it will go round.

Large sandwich loaf	($1\frac{3}{4}$ lb.) 20 slices
Larger sandwich loaf	($3\frac{1}{2}$ lb.) 50 slices
1 long French loaf	20 slices, about 1 in. per slice
6 oz. creamed butter	spreads 1 sandwich loaf $1\frac{3}{4}$ lb.
Salted nuts	$\frac{1}{2}$ oz. per person
Potato crisps	1 oz. per person
Cocktail snacks	5–6 per person

Sandwich Fillings

1 lb. cooked meat thinly sliced	fills 16 rounds of sandwiches
1 dozen chopped hard-boiled eggs with mayonnaise, etc.	fills 16 rounds of sandwiches
1 lb. grated cheese plus creamed butter, chives, etc.	fills 16 rounds of sandwiches
$1 \times 7\frac{3}{4}$-oz. can salmon flaked with mayonnaise, etc.	fills 4 rounds of sandwiches
Asparagus rolls	See page 201
1 lb. shortcrust pastry made with 1 lb. flour, 8 oz. fat, etc. will make	48 small pastry cases (using $2\frac{1}{2}$-in. cutter) 24 mince pies (using $2\frac{1}{2}$-in. cutter) 4×7-in. flan cases 3×8-in. flan cases 2×7-in. double pastry plate pie 2 steak and kidney pies, 2-pint oval dish
Meat for casserole	6 oz. per person

Joint with bone	6–8 oz. per person
without bone	4–6 oz. per person
Steak	6 oz. per person—hungry men 8 oz.
Sliced cold meat, i.e. ham, beef, pork	4 oz. per person
Chicken	$\frac{3}{4}$ lb.—1 lb. per person or, jointed, 1 joint i.e., leg or wing joint ($\frac{1}{4}$ chicken) per person
White fish	6 oz. per person
Salmon	4–5 oz. per person
Scampi	6–8 oz. per person
Sauces—Savoury	$\frac{1}{2}$ pint for four persons depending on sauce and dish
Soups	$\frac{1}{4}$–$\frac{1}{3}$ pint per person
Potatoes	$\frac{1}{2}$ lb. unpeeled per person
Peas	4–6 oz. prepared per person
Rice	1$\frac{1}{2}$–2 oz. uncooked per person
Spaghetti	3–4 oz. uncooked per person (if part of dish, e.g. Spaghetti Bolognese)
Strawberries	6 oz. per person
Raspberries	4 oz. per person
1 pint double cream to go with fruit salad	Serves 10–12
2 pints fruit salad	Serves 6–8
2-pint mould of cold mousse, i.e. orange	Serves 6–8
1 pint custard	Serves 4–6
7-in. Victoria Sandwich	Serves 6
9-in gâteau	Serves 8
Meringues: 6 egg whites, 12 oz. caster sugar, $\frac{3}{4}$ pint of cream, whipped	Make 24 pairs of meringues sandwiched together with cream

Drinks

Tea:	Allow $\frac{1}{3}$ pint per person
In small quantities	1 teaspoon in the pot per person
For numbers	2 oz. tea for 8 pints boiling water (for 25)

Milk to go with tea	2 pints for 25
Sugar to go with tea	1 lb. for 25
Coffee:	Allow $\frac{1}{3}$ pint per person
FRESH GROUND	
In small quantities	$1\frac{1}{2}$–2 oz. per pint water
For numbers	For 25: 8–10 oz. coffee 6 pints of water 3 pints of milk 1 lb. sugar

INSTANT	*Normal Strength*	*Stronger Coffee*
Per cup	1 teaspoon	1 heaped teaspoon
Per pint	1 heaped dessertspoon	1 rounded tablespoon
Per gallon	2 oz.	$2\frac{1}{2}$ oz.

Milk, etc. as above.

Wines and Spirits

Gin/Whisky	24 single measures per bottle
Sherry	12 glasses per bottle
Port	About 10–16 glasses per bottle
Liqueurs	About 32 small glasses per bottle
Bottle of wine	6–8 glasses 1 bottle for 4 diners 2 bottles for 6 diners
Champagne and sparkling wine	6–8 glasses per bottle
Beer	Can be bought in $\frac{1}{2}$ or 1 pint bottles. Cheaper in quantity for large numbers as 4-pint and 7-pint cans. A pin ($4\frac{1}{2}$ gallons) is the smallest sized barrel. Firkin (9 gallons)
Cider	Quart bottle—8 glasses
Pimms—1 bottle	1 bottle Pimms makes 16 half-pints when made up with splits of lemonade and ice or 32 Pimlets
Fruit squash	20 glasses per bottle
Mineral waters	1 large bottle serves two with gin/whisky, etc.

THE AMOUNT OF FOOD AND DRINK PER PERSON TO ALLOW FOR VARIOUS TYPES OF PARTIES

DRINKS PARTY

5–6 savouries
3–4 drinks

WEDDING RECEPTION/CHRISTENING/ENGAGEMENT PARTY

4–6 savouries (depending on size)
2 sweet items—éclairs/meringues/raspberries, etc.
1 piece wedding cake
3–4 drinks

CHILDREN'S TEA PARTY

4–6 savouries—sausages, crisps, open bridge rolls, cheese straws, small cheese biscuits, etc.
Ice-cream and chocolate biscuits
1 small piece of birthday cake
1 other cake or biscuit—sponge cake, chocolate fingers, etc.
2 cold drinks

TEENAGERS' PARTY

Either 1 main dish or three to five savouries
1 sweet dish
Cheese, celery and rolls
3–4 drinks

GROWN-UP TEA PARTY

4 small sandwiches or open bridge rolls
2 cakes or pastries
2 cups of tea

COFFEE MORNING

1 savoury
2 cakes or biscuits
2 cups of coffee

FORK BUFFET

1 starter
1 main dish
1 dessert or cheese
3–4 drinks

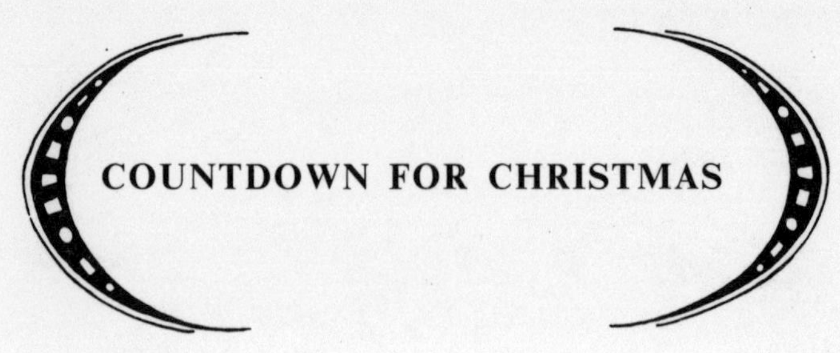

COUNTDOWN FOR CHRISTMAS

Each Christmas we vow to be more organized than last year, leaving time on Christmas morning to be free to be with the family. Get ahead by making clear-cut plans, starting with the count-up of the expected invasion of family and guests. I have chosen turkey as it is the most popular mainstay for the Christmas dinner. Being the largest of the birds there is plenty left over for other meals over the holiday. A twelve-pound bird will give altogether about twenty servings, depending on the generosity of the carver. The quantities given for the Christmas dinner are for six people and should be increased accordingly to suit your number of guests.

Christmas puddings (see page 143), mincemeat (see page 183) and the cake (see page 217) improve with keeping, so make them six to eight weeks before Christmas. A few extra puddings are ideal for presents or bazaars.

It is a good idea to make the cake, puddings and mincemeat on the same day, preparing and weighing the ingredients the day before. In this way all the shopping for dry goods is done in one go.

You know your own cooker, so take care not to bake the cake in too hot an oven; so many cakes are spoilt by burnt currants on top. If it shows signs of becoming too brown cover the top with a piece of brown paper. Store the baked Christmas cake wrapped in greaseproof paper, then foil or a cake tin, in a cool, dry larder or cupboard. Almond paste the cake four days to a week before putting on the white icing, which should be done just a day or so before Christmas.

CHRISTMAS DINNER MENU

Roast turkey
Roast potatoes
Bacon rolls
Chipolata sausages
Buttered sprouts
Glazed carrots
Chestnut stuffing
Lemon, thyme and sausage stuffing
Bread sauce
Christmas pudding
Mince pies
Rum sauce and brandy butter

GETTING READY FOR CHRISTMAS

By 23 December the puddings, mincemeat and cake will be made and even the mince pies can be baked a day or two earlier if it fits in better with your own timing. Here is a more detailed timetable for 23 December, Christmas Eve and Christmas Day.

23 DECEMBER

1. Make plenty of mince pies. Cool thoroughly then store in a cake tin in a cool larder.
2. Make breadcrumbs for bread sauce and stuffings.
3. Buy root vegetables, if these are not being delivered, and store in a dark, dry place.
4. If using a frozen turkey leave it to defrost in the refrigerator (it will take at least 48 hours).

CHRISTMAS EVE

1. Do all last-minute shopping as early in the day as possible.
2. Prepare the suggested stuffings. Wrap them individually in

greaseproof paper and foil and store them in a cool place or refrigerator. It is best not to stuff the bird until Christmas morning as if the weather is heavy the stuffings can go 'off'.

3. Prepare the bacon rolls but do not thread them on to skewers. Store in foil or an airtight container in the refrigerator.
4. Peel the vegetables. Cover the carrots and potatoes with cold water, wrap the onion in foil and put the sprouts in a polythene bag in the refrigerator.
5. Make the brandy butter and store it in the refrigerator or other cold place.

CHRISTMAS MORNING—Timing for Lunch at 1.30

9.30 Stuff turkey. Put it into a large meat tin. Heat oven to 350°F., Gas 4. Spread the breast of the turkey with 4 oz. butter, cover with rashers of streaky bacon and then cover the turkey loosely with foil.

9.45 Put the turkey in the oven. Put giblets, onions and seasonings in pan with water and simmer for gravy.

10.00 Put water on to boil for pudding—recipe page 210. Lay the table and coffee tray. Open cranberry sauce, if using bought, and put in sauce boat.

10.15 Put pudding on to boil, preferably in a steamer. Have a kettle of water on hand to top up the pan during the morning.
Next 1½ hours for Morning Service, a quick flip round with a duster, or whatever else has to be done.

12.00 Put salted water on to boil for potatoes. Melt fat in a second meat tin for roast potatoes. Heat onion and milk for bread sauce. Leave to infuse for half an hour.

12.15 Boil potatoes for 5 minutes then drain them and put in the hot fat. Roast at top of oven for 1 hour.

12.20 Make rum sauce. Leave in the pan, covered with buttered greaseproof paper so that a skin does not form.

12.30 Take foil off turkey, baste with fat and return to the oven uncovered.

12.40 Finish bread sauce and keep hot in a bowl standing over pan of rum sauce. Cover turkey legs with foil if they are beginning to brown.

12.45 Put carrots on to cook. Put dishes and plates in warming drawer of oven, in plate rack above cooker or in warming compartment above the oven.

12.55 Grill sausages for 10 minutes. Put bacon rolls on thin skewers and grill for 5 minutes. Keep both hot.

1.05 Put salted water on to boil for sprouts. Simmer them until tender, according to size. Drain them well and top with butter. Put into serving dish and keep hot.

1.15 Begin to dish up meal, remove turkey from oven. Leave to 'set' for 5 minutes before carving. Lower oven temperature to 300°F., Gas 2.

Put mince pies in oven to warm.

Drain carrots, add butter, put in a serving dish and sprinkle with nutmeg. Cover and keep warm.

1.20 Make gravy with the giblet stock, pour into gravy boat. Put bread sauce in serving dish and sprinkle with ground cloves, if liked.

1.25 Dish up turkey. Garnish with parsley or watercress. Put bacon rolls and sausages on a separate dish to make for easier carving. Turn the pudding on to a serving dish but do not remove the basin. Keep warm with mince pies at 300°F., Gas 2.

1.30 Serve Christmas dinner.

Roast Turkey

12-lb. dressed turkey; chestnut stuffing; lemon-sausage stuffing

Wipe the inside and outside of the bird with a clean, damp cloth. Stuff the neck end with chestnut stuffing, fold over the flap of skin and secure with a skewer. Stuff the tail end with lemon-sausage stuffing. Tie up the turkey with string. Put it in the meat tin, spread with butter and lay rashers of de-rinded streaky bacon over the breast. Cover it loosely with foil.

TIMES FOR ROASTING A TURKEY LOOSELY COVERED WITH FOIL

Weight after stuffing	*Cooking Time*	*Oven Temperature*
Up to 15 lb.	15 minutes per lb. plus 15 minutes extra time. Remove foil for last 30–40 minutes and baste.	350°F., Gas 4.
Over 15 lb.	12 minutes per lb. plus 12 minutes extra time. Remove foil for last 30–40 minutes and baste.	350°F., Gas 4.

Chestnut Stuffing

8-oz. can unsweetened chestnut purée, or 1 lb. chestnuts; 4 oz. fresh brown breadcrumbs; grated rind of ½ lemon; 1 large egg, beaten; 2 oz. butter, melted; salt; pepper

Preparation: see recipe *Cooking time: about 20 minutes*

Combine all the ingredients well, making sure that the stuffing is well seasoned with salt and pepper.

Note: If using fresh chestnuts make a slit in each one with a sharp knife, cook them in boiling water for 5 minutes and then remove the skins. Return them to the pan with just enough stock or water to cover and cook them for about 20 minutes or until they are tender. Drain them thoroughly, sieve or put them in the blender and use as above.

Lemon, Thyme and Sausage Stuffing

The turkey liver; 1 oz. butter; ¾ lb. pork sausage meat; 1 onion, peeled and finely chopped; ½ lb. fresh white breadcrumbs; 2–3 tablespoons chopped parsley; 1 level teaspoon dried thyme; grated rind and juice of 1 lemon; about 1 level teaspoon salt; ⅛ level teaspoon pepper; 1 egg, beaten

Preparation: 30 minutes

Chop the liver fairly finely and then fry it in the butter for 5 minutes. Add it to all the other ingredients and mix them thoroughly.

Bacon Rolls

6 streaky bacon rashers, de-rinded

Preparation: 10 minutes *Cooking time: about 5 minutes*

Stretch the rashers on a wooden board with the back of a knife until they are almost twice their original length. Cut each rasher in two. Roll up each piece. Place on thin skewers and grill for about 5 minutes until golden brown, turning once.

Roast Potatoes

2 lb. potatoes, peeled; 3 oz. lard

Preparation: 10 minutes *Cooking time: see page 210*

Cut the potatoes into even-sized pieces and then boil them in salted water for 5 minutes. Meanwhile melt the lard in a small meat tin above the turkey. Drain the potatoes well and turn them in the hot fat. Return to the oven (see 'Countdown').

Chipolata Sausages

1 lb. pork chipolata sausages

Preparation: 5 minutes *Cooking time: about 1¼ hours*

Prick the sausages well with a fork then grill them under a medium grill at the same time as the bacon rolls, turning the sausages so that they brown evenly.

Sprouts

2 lb. fresh sprouts

Preparation: 10 minutes *Cooking time: about 15 minutes*

Put the sprouts in boiling salted water and cook until they are tender, about 10–15 minutes, then drain them and toss in butter.

Glazed Carrots

$1\frac{1}{2}$ lb. carrots, peeled; $\frac{1}{2}$ oz. butter; salt; pepper; 1 teaspoon caster sugar
For topping: grated nutmeg; good knob butter; 1 tablespoon chopped parsley

Preparation: 10 minutes *Cooking time: about 40 minutes*

Cut the carrots into quarters lengthwise then put them into the pan with the butter, pepper, salt, sugar and just sufficient water to cover. Simmer them, covered, until they are tender then remove the lid and continue to simmer them until almost all the liquid has evaporated. Drain the carrots and turn them into a serving dish. Sprinkle with nutmeg, add more butter and scatter with parsley.

Rich Gravy

The turkey giblets, washed; two onions, peeled; 1 bay leaf; 1 sprig parsley; 1 blade of mace; $1\frac{1}{2}$ pints water; 2 tablespoons turkey fat; 1 oz. flour; salt; pepper; 3 tablespoons sherry; gravy browning

Preparation: 10 minutes *Cooking time: about 10 minutes*

Put the giblets into a pan with the onions, bay leaf, parsley, mace and water. Cover the pan with a tightly fitting lid, bring the liquor to the boil and simmer for about 3 hours. Strain.

Put the turkey fat into a pan, blend in the flour and cook the roux over a low heat, stirring all the time, until it has turned brown. Add the giblet stock a little at a time, blending it until it is smooth. Bring it to the boil and simmer for 2 minutes until it has thickened. Season with salt and pepper, stir in the sherry and add a few drops of gravy browning if necessary to make the gravy a rich brown colour.

Bread Sauce

1 onion, peeled; 2 cloves; ½ pint milk; 2 oz. fresh white breadcrumbs; salt; pepper; ½ oz. butter

Preparation: 5 minutes *Cooking time: about 35 minutes*

Put the onion, stuck with the cloves, into a pan with the milk. Heat it gently to boiling point then turn off the heat and leave it to infuse for 30 minutes. Remove the onion and cloves from the pan and stir in the breadcrumbs, seasoning and butter. Re-heat the sauce almost to boiling point and then cover with damp greaseproof paper and keep warm until required.

Rum Sauce

1 oz. butter; 1 oz. flour; ½ pint milk; 1 oz. caster sugar; 3–4 tablespoons rum

Preparation: 10 minutes *Cooking time: about 10 minutes*

Melt the butter in a small pan then remove it from the heat and blend in the flour. Return the pan to the heat and cook the roux gently for 1 minute. Add the milk a little at a time, blending it until it is smooth. Stir in the sugar and then simmer the sauce for 2–3 minutes until it has thickened, stirring all the time. Add the rum and then keep the sauce covered with a piece of buttered, moistened greaseproof paper until it is required so that a skin does not form.

Brandy Butter

3 oz. unsalted butter; 6 oz. icing sugar, sieved; 2–3 tablespoons brandy

Preparation: 15 minutes

Beat the butter until it is soft then add the icing sugar and continue to beat until the mixture is light and fluffy. Beat in the brandy then turn the brandy butter into a serving dish and leave it in the refrigerator to harden before using. Take it out of the refrigerator at least half an hour before serving.

Mince Pies

MAKES 12

For the rich shortcrust pastry: 8 oz. plain flour; ½ level teaspoon salt; 3 oz. butter; 2 oz. lard; 1 egg, separated; about 2 teaspoons cold water.

A jar of mincemeat; a little caster sugar

Preparation: 35 minutes *Cooking time: about 35 minutes*

Get out a 12-holed patty tin.

Set oven at 400°F., Gas 6.

This amount just makes twelve, so you may like to double up on the quantities if you are expecting a number of visitors over Christmas.

Rub the fats into the flour in the usual way, blend the egg yolk with 2 teaspoons cold water then mix it with the rubbed-in mixture to make a firm dough. If necessary add a few extra drops of cold water. Roll the pastry out thinly on a well-floured board and cut it into 12 rounds with a 2¾-in. pastry cutter. Re-roll the remaining pastry if necessary and cut it into 12 rounds with a 3¼-in. fluted cutter. Put the large rounds of pastry into the patty tins and prick the bases with a fork. Fill each patty tin with a heaped teaspoon of mincemeat, moisten the edges of the pastry with water and top with a smaller circle of pastry. Make two small cuts on top of the pies and bake them for 10 minutes then remove them from the oven, brush them with the lightly-beaten egg white, sprinkle with caster sugar and bake them for a further 15 minutes or until they are golden brown.

Hot Claret Punch

MAKES 24 GLASSFULS

1 lemon; 2 bottles cheap claret; 4 sherry glassfuls sherry; 1 sherry glassful port; 1 pint water; 1 stick cinnamon; 12 cloves, tied in muslin; 1 sherry glassful brandy; 2–4 oz. caster sugar

Preparation: 15 minutes *Cooking time: about 15 minutes*

This is a good punch to have for any chilly evening. If you are keeping it hot over a long period do see that it doesn't boil or the flavour will be lost.

Peel the lemon thinly and squeeze out the juice. Put the claret, sherry, port, water, cinnamon stick, cloves and lemon peel into a pan. Bring this slowly to the boil and simmer gently for 15 minutes. Then remove the cinnamon stick, cloves and peel and add the juice of the lemon, brandy and sugar to taste. Serve piping hot.

Christmas Cake

9 oz. plain flour; $\frac{1}{4}$ level teaspoon salt; 1 level teaspoon mixed spice; 8 oz. butter; 8 oz. soft brown sugar; 4 eggs; $1\frac{1}{2}$ level tablespoons black treacle; 2 lb. mixed dried fruit (raisins, sultanas, currants); 4 oz. glacé cherries, quartered; 4 oz. candied peel, chopped; 2 oz. almonds, blanched and chopped; 2 tablespoons brandy for adding when cake is baked

Preparation: $1\frac{1}{2}$ hours *Cooking time: about 4 hours*

Get out 8-in. diameter cake tin

Set oven at 300°F., Gas 2.

This Christmas cake isn't elaborately piped with an abundance of roses and motifs, yet it has the real feel of Christmas and is quick and easy. The sides and top are iced in peaky royal icing. The holly leaves are home-made from the almond paste trimmings.

Line an 8-in. diameter cake tin with a double thickness of greaseproof paper. Sift together the flour, salt and mixed spice. Cream butter and sugar until light and creamy. Beat in black treacle. Add eggs, one at a time, beating each in thoroughly and adding one tablespoon of flour with every egg. Fold in remaining flour. Add

CHRISTMAS CAKE—GUIDE TC

INGREDIENTS	ROUND TIN: *6 inch* SQUARE TIN: *5 inch*	*7 inch* *6 inch*
Basic Rich Cake Mixture		
Butter	4 oz.	6 oz.
Soft Brown Sugar	4 oz.	6 oz.
Eggs	2	3
Plain Flour	5 oz.	7 oz.
Salt	Pinch	Pinch
Black Treacle	½ tablesp.	1 tablesp.
Mixed Dried Fruit	1 lb.	1½ lb.
Candied Peel	2 oz.	3 oz.
Cherries	2 oz.	3 oz.
Chopped Almonds	½ oz.	1 oz.
Mixed Spice	¼ level teasp.	½ level teasp.
Brandy	1 tablesp.	2 tablesp.
Almond Paste—Sufficient for Top and Sides		
Ground Almonds	8 oz.	10 oz.
Caster Sugar	4 oz.	5 oz.
Icing Sugar	4 oz.	5 oz.
Almond Essence	Few Drops	Few Drops
Egg Yolks	2	3
Lemon Juice	1 tablesp.	2 tablesp.
Royal Icing		
Icing Sugar	1 lb.	1 lb.
Egg Whites	2	2
Lemon Juice	½ teasp.	½ teasp.
Glycerine	1 teasp.	1 teasp.

BAKING TIMES

6–7-in. cake 300°F., Gas 2 for 2 hours. Lower to 250°F., Gas ½ for about 1½ hours.

8–9-in. cake 300°F., Gas 2 for 3 hours. Lower to 250°F., Gas ½ for about 1 hour.

10–12-in. cake 300°F., Gas 2 for 3¼ hours. Lower to 250°F., Gas ½ for about 1–2 hours

TIN SIZE AND RECIPE QUANTITIES

TIN SIZE

8 inch *7 inch*	*9 inch* *8 inch*	*10 inch* *9 inch*	*11 inch* *10 inch*	*12 inch* *11 inch*
8 oz.	10 oz.	12 oz.	14 oz.	1 lb.
8 oz.	10 oz.	12 oz.	14 oz.	1 lb.
4	5	6	7	8
9 oz.	11 oz.	13 oz.	15 oz.	1 lb. 1 oz.
¼ level teasp.	¼ level teasp.	½ level teasp.	½ level teasp.	¾ level teasp.
1½ tablesp.	2 tablesp.	2½ tablesp.	3 tablesp.	3½ tablesp.
2 lb.	2½ lb.	3 lb.	3½ lb.	4 lb.
4 oz.	5 oz.	6 oz.	7 oz.	8 oz.
4 oz.	5 oz.	6 oz.	7 oz.	8 oz.
2 oz.	3 oz.	4 oz.	5 oz.	6 oz.
1 level teasp.	1½ level teasp.	2 level teasp.	2½ level teasp.	3 level teasp.
2 tablesp.	3 tablesp.	3 tablesp.	4 tablesp.	4 tablesp.
12 oz.	12 oz.	14 oz.	14 oz.	1 lb.
6 oz.	6 oz.	7 oz.	7 oz.	8 oz.
6 oz.	6 oz.	7 oz.	7 oz.	8 oz.
¼ teasp.	¼ teasp.	½ teasp.	½ teasp.	¾ teasp.
4	4	5	5	6
3 tablesp.	3 tablesp.	4 tablesp.	4 tablesp.	5 tablesp.
1½ lb.	1½ lb.	2 lb.	2 lb.	2½ lb.
3	3	4	4	5
1 teasp.	1 teasp.	1½ teasp.	1½ teasp.	2 teasp.
1½ teasp.	1½ teasp.	2 teasp.	2 teasp.	2½ teasp.

dried fruit, glacé cherries, chopped peel and chopped almonds and mix well. Place mixture in lined tin, make a hollow in centre about 1 in. deep and bake the cake in centre of a warm oven, 300°F., Gas 2 for 3 hours then reduce temperature to 250°F., Gas ½, for a further hour or so until cooked. Cover cake with a layer of brown paper if top is becoming too brown. To test if cake is done, push a skewer into the middle of cake—it will come out clean if cake is cooked. Leave at least 20 minutes before turning out of tin. Cool on a wire rack. When the cake is nearly cold spoon brandy over the top and let it soak in. When quite cold wrap well in greaseproof paper then kitchen foil and store in an airtight tin for at least a month, if possible, in a cool dry larder.

Christmas Cake Icing

For the almond paste: ¾ lb. ground almonds; 6 oz. icing sugar, sieved; 6 oz. caster sugar; 4 egg yolks; few drops almond essence
For the apricot glaze: about 3 tablespoons apricot jam, sieved
For the royal icing: 4 egg whites; 2 lb. icing sugar, sieved; 2 teaspoons lemon juice; 2 teaspoons glycerine
To decorate the cake: Green, blue and red vegetable colouring; 10-in. diameter silver cake board; a red candle or any bought decoration such as Father Christmas on sleigh

First prepare the almond paste. Mix together the ground almonds and sugars in a bowl then add just enough of the egg yolk to bind the mixture together. Do not add too much egg or the mixture will be soft and sticky. Add a few drops of almond essence and then knead the almond paste in the bowl until it is smooth. Form the paste into a round and then cut off one-third of it. Roll this smaller piece out on a board which has been lightly dusted with icing sugar to form an 8-in. circle (use the cake tin as a guide). Brush the top of the cake with apricot glaze, and if necessary, build up the edges of the cake with some of the remaining paste so that the top is flat. Turn the cake on to the circle of almond paste and press it firmly so that the almond paste sticks to the cake, then turn the cake the right way up and put it on the wooden board.

Measure the circumference of the cake with a piece of string and then measure the depth with a ruler. Roll out the remaining paste, reserving a piece about the size of a golf ball for making the holly leaves, to form two strips, each exactly half the circumference and the same depth as the cake. Brush the sides of the cake with apricot glaze and press the strips round the sides of the cake, smoothing the two joins with a round-bladed knife so that they are firmly sealed. Leave the cake on a board for at least 4 days to dry out the almond paste.

Just before Christmas ice the cake. Prepare the royal icing. Put the egg whites into a bowl and whisk them with a fork until they are frothy. Add the sieved icing sugar a tablespoon at a time and beat the icing well after each addition. When about two-thirds of the icing sugar has been added beat the icing really well for about 5 minutes (this helps to make the icing white). Stir in the lemon juice and glycerine and then beat in the remaining icing sugar. Put a little icing on to the silver cake board and stand the cake on top. Practise drawing up the icing in peaks with a palette knife. If the icing is too stiff to do this add a few drops of water to soften it. Spread the icing thickly round the sides then the top of the cake, a few inches at a time, and make peaks in the icing with a palette knife as you go. Put the cake on one side to set overnight.

Take about a quarter of the remaining almond paste and flatten it into a circle with the fingers. Put a few drops of red vegetable colouring on to the paste and then knead the paste until it is an even red. Add a few more drops of colouring if necessary. Roll the paste into small balls to resemble holly berries and then set them on one side to dry.

Colour the remaining paste in the same way, using green vegetable colouring and a very little blue to make the paste dark green. Roll it out on a board lightly dusted with icing sugar until it is about $\frac{1}{16}$ in. thick. Using a ruler as a guide cut the paste into 1-in. wide strips and then cut the strips into diamonds. Use the base of an icing nozzle or the cap of a fountain pen to remove small half-circles from the sides of the diamonds to form holly leaves. Make 'vein' marks on the leaves with the tip of a sharp knife and then bend the leaves over the handles of wooden spoons to dry.

When the icing on the cake has set hard, put the candle on top of the cake on a base of a little stiff royal icing and then arrange the holly leaves and berries round the base of the candle. Arrange the remaining holly leaves and berries round the sides of the cake, securing them with royal icing.

INDEX